Changing Managers and Managing Change

Mahmoud Ezzamel
Chris Green
Simon Lilley
Hugh Willmott
(Manchester School of Management, UMIST)

The Chartered Institute of Management Accountants
63 Portland Place
London W1N 4AB

First published in 1995 by:

The Chartered Institute of Management Accountants

ISBN 1 874784 35 3

The publisher of this book considers that it is a worthwhile contribution to discussion, without necessarily sharing the views expressed, which are those of the authors.

No responsibility for loss occasioned to any person acting or refraining from action as a result of any material in this publication can be accepted by the authors or publisher.

Contents

Acknowledgements

We wish to thank CIMA for the funding that made this research possible and for the continued support and encouragement of the Institute throughout the project.

The research team, all based at the Manchester School of Management, UMIST, comprised Mahmoud Ezzamel, Price Waterhouse Professor of Accounting and Finance, Simon Lilley, ESRC Management Teaching Fellow, and Hugh Willmott, Reader in Organisational Analysis. The research results reported here are based on the questionnaire and interviews undertaken by these three authors and previously written up in an end of award research report. Chris Green, Forum Director of the Financial Services Research Centre, joined the team and was put in charge of rewriting the end of award research report to obtain this final report. We should also like to thank Ms Liz Goddard for her secretarial input in transcribing interview tapes and preparing drafts.

In addition, we should like to acknowledge the assistance of the Financial Services Research Centre (FSRC) at UMIST and the continued support and encouragement of many colleagues.

We also wish to thank and acknowledge all those anonymous managers in many organisations who responded to our questionnaire and who willingly gave up much valuable time during lengthy in-depth interviews. The insights we gained and the findings we present would not be possible without such invaluable co-operation, for which we are indebted.

However, the views and interpretations we express here are our responsibility, not necessarily being those of any individual or organisation who participated in the study, nor those of CIMA. We take full responsibility for any errors or omissions in the report and welcome any comments, suggestions or other feedback from managers, after they have considered this report and our findings.

Executive Summary

This management report reviews a large-scale project carried out by the authors during 1992 and 1993. The research was funded by the Chartered Institute of Management Accountants (CIMA), the objective being to:

> Provide a systematic study of management practices, and especially the changes that have taken place in recent years and their impacts on the potential and actual use of management accounting. Identify major changes in management philosophy and practice over the past decade and the possible future directions.

This multidisciplinary study therefore adds to the many books and articles about management change that have proliferated over the past decade. Much of this output is prescriptive and often contradictory, as the latest fashionable trend is promoted. In contrast, this report is based firmly on empirical research to document changes and to then offer an informed, practical explanation of their dynamics. Our premise is that much of the superficially attractive rhetoric of management gurus should be critically challenged, but that such informed debate requires a combination of evidence, theory and analysis, which this report seeks to provide.

Through this empirical research and review of recent developments in organisational analysis, our intention is to help managers, especially those involved with accounting, to better understand management change. In the text we are careful to introduce theoretical concepts in a practical way, illustrated by examples recognisably drawn from the real world. The research will therefore be relevant to the way managers operate now and how they may better manage the challenges of future change.

The first introductory chapter provides an overview of the research, outlining our objectives and motivations together with the research methods used, and concludes with a review of the salient findings on which our broad conclusions and recommendations are based. The report draws upon a wide range of case study material, built upon 62 in-depth interviews. These supplement an earlier extensive questionnaire, with 129 respondents from a wide cross-section of UK corporations. All seven chapters are essentially self-contained, concentrating on the research findings and clearly focused on specific but broad themes. This enables the reader to 'dip into' the study, for particular areas of interest and relevance to them, without having to read the entire account.

Chapter 2 outlines the questions and reports the significant responses. Our interpretation yields some interesting insights into the general process of change in UK management practices. From the top of UK organisations, managers were seen to be responding to intensified competition, but these demands were translated for the lower managerial echelons into increased attention to issues of quality and the introduction of computer technology.

However, across all levels the most significant change was a greater pressure for results. Taken as a whole, this led us to conclude that, although there is indeed much evidence of extensive organisational change, there was little in our survey findings to support more grandiose claims about a sea change in management. The changes appear to be those of degree, rather than any more radical break with past practice.

Chapter 3 draws mainly on the interview data. In this chapter we discuss and criticise new wave management theories. We consider whether there has actually been the expected transformation of management style from the traditional 'command and control' to the new organisation based on 'facilitate and empower'. The evidence does suggest that UK managers are committed to the sorts of changes advocated by the new wave gurus, but we also found they had a much keener sense of the practical limitations that are not admitted by the leading proponents. In many ways quite orthodox command and control changes appeared to be dressed up in the new wave language.

Chapter 4 develops earlier arguments, with particular reference to flexibility, and highlights some of the contradictions and tensions identified in previous chapters, including notions of individualism and collectivism. The data suggests that UK managers encourage team working through differential packages of individual incentives.

We also show how managers take advantage of the economic recession, high unemployment and a weakened trade union movement to introduce practices that have been derived from a very different context. We again conclude that in many cases the command and control style organisation seems to live on beneath the surface of the new wave management methods.

Chapter 5 begins with an introduction which explains the concepts of HRM and reviews its background, so we feel that all managers will find this section particularly useful. The nature of HRM and its strategic role in organisational change are examined, including employee involvement and team working. We look at how HRM practices may strengthen managerial prerogative through the reduction of worker resistance, and use our data to show the changes, continuities and contradictions in HRM. We suggest that it would be a mistake to conclude that enlightened HRM policies and practices were a cause of any new understanding between employers and employees. Tensions and conflict in the employment relationship seem to us to have been temporarily subdued by the external context, but not permanently removed.

Chapter 6 looks again at some of the sectoral differences first identified in Chapter 2, by exploring the peculiarities of changes in management practice in financial services organisations. This is a sector where very long-established structures and comfortable practices were radically upset in the mid-1980s by deregulation through the Financial Services Act.

In the financial services firms we researched there was more evidence of the empowerment of managerial staff, but ironically those managers that remained were being empowered to manage their subordinates more intensively.

In Chapter 7 we draw together the research findings to reflect on the implications and challenges of organisational change for the management accounting function and its practices. After hinting, in broad terms, at the extent to which the role of management accounting in organisations is perceived to be changing we then examine the relationship between accounting and empowerment, accountability, motivation and remuneration, to suggest how management accounting might respond differently, for there seems to be little or no evidence of a basic change of emphasis in the accounting function.

However, if the gurus and their managerial supporters are to be believed, it is just such a change that the new organisation requires.

1 Introduction

This report is intended to help any manager involved with organisational change. It reviews a research project funded by the Chartered Institute of Management Accountants (CIMA), and carried out by the authors in two phases during 1992 and 1993. The objectives of the study were to:

> Provide a systematic study of management practices, and especially the changes that have taken place in recent years and their impacts on the potential and actual use of management accounting. Identify major changes in management philosophy and practice over the past decade and the possible future directions.

In this introductory chapter we first explain why we wanted to carry out this research and broadly define the empirical data we were seeking. The next section briefly outlines how the study was planned and the research methods used. This explains why we combined survey and interview data collection and how this sought to fill an identified gap in the literature.

1.1 *The research study: motivation and objectives*

Many commentators agree that the 1980s was a decade of unprecedented organisational change and that competition is now increasingly and significantly more intense and more international, e.g., the penetration of leading Japanese and Western European companies, and the gaining of larger export shares. In the UK domestic competition has also been fuelled by a deep economic recession. We quantify and qualify these ideas, and provide supporting empirical evidence.

Changes in management practice are both a condition and a consequence of such increasing competition and the restructuring of national and international markets. Some influential writers argue that organisational change is part and parcel of a bigger change in advanced capitalist societies, as established economic and social institutions are progressively eroded and disorganised. However, our research does not lend too much support to such grand claims.

In the face of increased uncertainty managers have developed various aggressive and defensive strategies to improve their competitive positions. These include mergers and acquisitions, rationalisation through internal reorganisation, centralisation of critical functions, outsourcing and cost containment, and using new administrative and accounting procedures. At the same time, advances in manufacturing and information technologies (IT) have significantly altered the pattern and structure of work flows.

This combination of factors has resulted in a redefinition of significant aspects of the managerial function. Other IT innovations, particularly in artificial intelligence (AI), decision support systems (DSS) and management information systems (MIS), have also been involved in a reassessment of managerial roles and of established horizontal and vertical relationships within the organisation. Evidence suggests there is an unprecedented corporate upheaval, but as writers diagnose and report this they simultaneously promote change as a good thing for its own sake.

A new breed of influential management guru has emerged, stressing the importance of improving flexibility, strengthening culture and enhancing quality, through change. They say this is necessary to compete successfully in markets that are increasingly global in scope. High market penetration has been taken as evidence of the superior practices of the Japanese, and Western managers have been encouraged to emulate them. Perhaps the best-known popular example of many such books is Peters and Waterman (1982).

Companies are advised that to survive and prosper they must become leaner and more responsive. In particular they must be more adaptable and oriented to continuous change and renewal. So managers are urged to:

- become closer to their customers and market driven;
- de-layer what are now deemed to be redundant levels of their

organisation's hierarchies, promote multi-skilling and apply new technologies;
- improve the quality and responsiveness of their activities, but also reduce costs.

This large and increasing body of literature both advocates the desirability of change and prescribes its implementation, ideas that are now being questioned and critically evaluated. The new management gurus are being challenged that their prescriptive writings and quick-fix solutions:

- are invariably evangelical and focused exclusively on successes;
- tend to exclude any doubt and reflection on the plausibility of their assumptions;
- offer little or no evidence of the practicalities and implications of implementation.

However, the analytical criticism is usually aimed at an academic audience and often concerns theoretical aspects of the debate, so it lacks popular appeal and is not a much-desired solution. Some small case studies of the effects of organisational change have been published, but managers have little general and systematic evidence of the experience in firms that have tried to implement the new wave of management ideas. While academic attention has been devoted to debating the theoretical significance of the changes, relatively little effort has been applied to conducting empirical research to identify the nature and extent of such change, as Wood (1989) observed:

> Detailed case studies of firms which have made major changes are vitally needed.... They should deal with the changing nature of the political and career systems which develop under the new management regimes, as organisations attempt to transform themselves in the image of the new wave.

Thus a number of key questions concerning the nature and impact of these developments on managerial work remain, and the research reported in the following chapters attempts to partially rectify this imbalance. We report the extent of 'new' management thinking concerning change and the experiences of managers, who are both the subjects and objects of its implementation.

1.2 Research method

Our study of changing management practices consisted of two phases:

1. A 1992 questionnaire survey of 129 UK private-sector companies, to enquire about the extent to which new management ideas have been embraced.
2. A subsequent series of 62 interviews with senior and middle managers from 27 of these companies, selected on the basis of their survey responses and their agreement to allow research access.

The survey was designed to generate cross-sectoral data on perceived changes in management practice. A lengthy and detailed questionnaire was sent to the chief executives of companies drawn from *The Times Top 1000* companies, and other financial services organisations. It was either completed by the CEO himself or delegated to other directors or senior managers. The industrial classification of responding organisations is given in Table 1.1 below:

Table 1.1 Industrial classification of questionnaire replies

Industrial classification	Questionnaire replies
Capital goods	26
Consumer goods (durable)	17
Consumer goods (non-durable)	14
Chemicals and pharmaceuticals	9
Extractive industries	4
Utilities	5
Financial services	31
Other	23
Total	129

The survey covered a wide range of topics and included a number of open-ended questions. Respondents were asked to rate the importance of factors in fostering change, for the UK corporate sector as a whole and in their own organisations. They were also asked to specify which of the factors had been most important for changes in top, middle, and junior management. Finally, they were given an opportunity to provide their own descriptions of how management practice had changed within their own organisations.

The second phase, of 62 detailed interviews in 27 organisations, yielded richer qualitative data, to enable us to check and expand the survey findings. The breadth of organisations and managers covered by this phase of the research enabled the survey and case study based research to be linked.

Since the questionnaire imposed a common language, one objective was to verify the apparent similarity of many answers. The interviews revealed a diversity of management practices in ways that survey research alone cannot.

However, balancing this is a weakness resulting from the research design favoured by our sponsors, which excluded interviews with non-managerial employees. We were also asked to visit a comparatively large (20 per cent) sample of respondents, who were geographically dispersed around the country. Time and cost constraints therefore restricted the interview schedule, and consequently there were few opportunities to cross-check the accounts with other managers, or shop-floor subordinates.

Notwithstanding these qualifications and criticisms, we believe the research does illuminate, even if only partially, the way managers interpret changes in their work and organisation, providing insights into the complexities of implementing new policies. The evidence suggests that those managers who display an ardent and seemingly naïve enthusiasm for new wave management are matched by others who embrace it cynically and appear highly sceptical about many of its claims. We consider whether these differences reflect the extent to which these ideas are established and operating effectively within different organisations.

Alternatively, the diversity of views might be an example of a public relations concern, as some managers seemed exceptionally keen to display their knowledge of the latest management fashions. Others, perhaps also concerned to demonstrate their credentials, presented more cautious or even critical evaluations of the latest fad. This contextually dependent nature of interview accounts cannot be disregarded, and it would have been valuable to have developed greater rapport with our interviewees by making more return visits.

Despite this, we believe the data tell us something about managers' genuine but guarded perceptions of how new wave policies and practices are operating within their organisations. Our interview findings have both expanded the survey responses and also been qualified by them. For example, the questionnaire answers suggest that some practices claimed by some interviewees to be widespread are, in fact, rather limited in their application. With this combined evidence, it is possible to build up a broad picture of the manager's perceptions of the nature, significance and impact of recent changes in UK organisations. We then examine this data from particular perspectives.

Other surveys, particularly those commissioned by the Institute of Management (IM), formerly the British Institute of Management (BIM), also provide some basis for generalisation and comparison but, being limited to members, their sample population is more restricted.

We have also attempted to be more critical, by including probing questions about management practices and philosophies, which are noticeably absent from other surveys that we have examined.

The industrial classification of the organisations where we conducted interviews, and the job designation of interviewees, are given in Tables 1.2 and 1.3.

Table 1.2 Industrial classification by number of organisations

Industrial classification	Number of organisations
Capital goods	4
Consumer goods (durable)	4
Consumer goods (non-durable)	3
Chemicals and pharmaceuticals	4
Extractive industries	1
Utilities	2
Financial services	6
Other manufacturing	3
Total	27

Table 1.3 Job designation of interviewees

Job designation	Number interviewed
Chairman	1
Chief operating officer	2
Vice president	1
Finance director	10
Managing director	8
Human resources director[1]	7
Manufacturing director	3
Quality and systems director	1
Financial controller[2]	7
Human resources manager[3]	7
General manager	2
Assistant general manager	4
Production manager[4]	4
Information technology manager	1
Department manager	1
National sales manager	1
Strategic planning manager	2
Total	62

Notes to Table 3

1. 'Human resource director' includes the job titles of 'employee relations director' and 'personnel director'.
2. Includes other senior finance job titles, but not directors
3. See note 1.
4. Includes job titles of 'plant manager' and 'operations manager'.

1.3 Main findings and conclusions

Many publications seek to teach and reassure managers that strategic change can be successfully managed by adopting the latest recipe. Little research, however, examines the associated practical difficulties, not least because managers and consultants are reluctant to admit failure publicly, even though this would be instructive to others. We thus only read the success stories. We suggest that the pundits, in offering quick-fix solutions, often overlook significant problems of implementation.

They perhaps also conveniently minimise the influence of the external contexts in which changes are taking place. We draw attention to the danger of assuming that any latest management technique has created a permanent change; this may prove to be temporary as the external context shifts yet again. Supported by the research evidence we are therefore critical of simplistic approaches to change and to the notion of a major transformation in management techniques. We find managers are rightly sceptical of the evangelical exhortations to change radically, and often show a much greater understanding of the complex implications than do the experts and consultants.

While flexibility is a dominant concept, it seems doubtful if this idea alone is adequate to grasp fully the complexity, diversity and potential tensions implicit in organisational changes. The evidence is that 'accountability', 'results' and 'quality' are of equal or greater importance as watchwords of contemporary change.

We conclude that changes appear to be those of degree, rather than a radical break with past practice. The picture is one of intensification and individualisation of work, facilitated by new technology and promoted by ideas like HRM and TQM. There appears to be a strong appreciation of the importance of the human resource when managing change, but as yet no adequate solutions to the inherent tensions of HRM policies and practices. Changing systems, structures and techniques is necessary, but not sufficient, to successfully implement the new organisation.

2
How Has Management Changed?

2.1 Introduction

In the previous chapter we outlined how the questionnaire would identify senior managerial perceptions of the extent to which organisations have been transformed and how this has been achieved. We now present the key findings under a number of sub-headings, but omit statistical tests. We conclude that rapid and continuous change has been taking place in UK companies and that this has been facilitated by developments in the wider economic context. We note that tensions are developing between a taken-for-granted emphasis on individualism and the current fashion for teams and networking. However, we find such changes to team work are changes of degree, rather than a quantum break with established management practices.

2.2 Background

Whittaker (1992) reviewed recent major studies of contemporary organisational change. These identify a dramatic decline in manufacturing employment, a boom in the financial sector and an expansion in services associated with outsourcing. Part-time female workers have increased, particularly in new areas specialising in data handling and information processing. A polarised workforce is developing with tensions evident between an élite core and those part-time, casual and short-term contract workers at the periphery. Whittaker concludes that the 1980s were a decade of 'quantum organisational change, much of it focusing on the pursuit of flexibility'. But there are two points that strike us about this claim.

1. Despite reference to certain studies, there is a little supporting evidence.

2. There are conspicuous gaps in our knowledge about the direction and scope of the changes that are deemed to have occurred, although a few intensive case studies do provide a better understanding of their processes.

This lack of evidence may partly be due to the limitations of survey research and an understandable scepticism about whether this can produce factual answers to questions about the nature and extent of organisational change. Rather than face the difficulty of identifying and agreeing what the relevant facts are, therefore, it is tempting instead to engage in debates about ideas and concepts. Thus researchers consider the meaning and reality of a concept like 'flexibility', rather than undertake surveys that are fraught with difficulties, not least being the pressure to produce a respectable response rate.

2.3 Accounts of changing management practice

Research studies of organisational restructuring and changing management practice divide into two broad approaches.

2.3.1 Case studies

A case study captures the richness and ambiguity of management practices to present an account of significant change, e.g., technology, job design, organisational structure, product markets and corporate structure. Pettigrew's (1985) study of ICI is a good example. Others include Whipp and Clark (1986) at Rover; Clark et al. (1988) at BT; Smith et al. (1991) at Cadbury's. Knights and Willmott (1993) also review organisational change at a medium-sized financial services company.

The value of these studies is their detailed analysis, often over a long period, of the process and politics of organisational change. By focusing upon a particular company, or a specific set of issues within a company, they are able to examine the dynamics of change and provide penetrating insights into organisational complexity and how to manage change. This helps to develop an understanding of organisational change that may have broader or general relevance.

2.3.2 Surveys or questionnaires

While case studies make important contributions to a general theory of managerial work or organisational change, it is not plausible to generalise on the evidence drawn from one, or even a limited number. Surveys are a more convenient, but still imperfect, foundation for generalisations as, despite considerable limitations, they can generate data from a large number of different organisations. On the basis of such evidence it is possible to ascertain perceptions of the nature and significance of recent changes in UK organisations.

The Institute of Management (IM), formerly the British Institute of Management (BIM), are major sponsors of survey research, having commissioned surveys on various aspects of organisational change: e.g., Peppercorn and Skoulding (1987); Coulson-Thomas and Brown (1989, 1990); Coulson-Thomas and Coe (1991) and Wheatley (1992). These IM/BIM member surveys have consistently indicated that change in organisations during the past decade has been rapid and widespread.

Table 2.1 Key IM/BIM findings

80 per cent of managers are reported to have experienced one or more corporate restructurings in their organisations in the last five years. *(Wheatley, 1992)*
90 per cent of the organisations were becoming 'slimmer and flatter'. *(Coulson-Thomas and Coe, 1991)*
75 per cent of the managers who had experienced restructuring reported increases in their workload and responsibility. Teamwork and generalist skills were reported to be increasing in importance, especially for middle managers. *(Wheatley, 1992)*
79 per cent of managers were undertaking more work in teams.
67 per cent said functions are becoming more interdependent, with procedure and permanency being replaced by flexibility and temporary arrangements. *(Coulson-Thomas and Coe, 1991)*

2.3.3 *Our findings*

The IM/BIM conclusions are supported by our survey but, compared with our study, the IM research was narrower in scope and less obviously informed by relevant organisational change literature. Thus, although there is an overlap, there are differences in approach. We may speculate that the IM concern was to generate data about the perceptions of their members, perhaps to present an Institute view, as well as contribute to policy debates and influence key decision-makers. In contrast, we wanted answers to questions and concerns arising from earlier academic research.

At the same time, we anticipated that potential respondents, and the practitioners reading this report, would not react favourably to academic jargon or theoretical debates. We therefore made our questions direct and accessible, testing them with a pilot questionnaire, though this meant an unavoidable compromise. We wanted to develop a comprehensive survey of the diversity and complexity of organisational change, but not to make the questionnaire excessively long. However, a few respondents suggested we were too demanding in length, if not in content. This may explain the 13 per cent response rate, which is typical for very long questionnaires.

2.4 *Survey design: strengths and limitations*

The survey covered a wide range of topics and included a number of open-ended questions. In general, the questions were more discriminating than those asked of IM members, and put to a wider sample. We also included a much larger number of factors when asking managers to identify the nature and scope of changes, and the pressures perceived by them to promote change. A total of 129 usable questionnaires were returned.

Using both survey and case study approaches, our complete report provides a generalised view of changes in management practice. We included a number of more probing questions, usually absent from other surveys, and questions not obviously and directly relevant to the immediate concerns of managers. This research design was to enable us to obliquely and indirectly examine the subtle issues relevant to organisational change.

Negatively, it could reasonably be asked, 'How representative is the respondent sample and the questionnaire?' In common with the IM surveys, respondents were senior executives, working mainly in large and medium-sized firms. Public-sector organisations were not surveyed. It may also be questioned whether such surveys develop a picture of changing management practice, or simply represent the opinions of a subset of people who, for unknown reasons, are more willing to respond to 'academic' surveys.

Most fundamentally, it must be acknowledged that the survey data present perceptions, not necessarily reflections of reality. For example, when we identify factors that have been most important in fostering change among middle or junior managers, we are reporting senior managers' perceptions of changes. When considering such criticism of this and any other survey data, it is worth recalling that all observations must inevitably be mediated by our perceptions. It is simply impossible to access and mirror the 'raw facts'.

Even data produced by participant observation of change processes are mediated by the researcher's prior prejudices, however 'objectively' they may be presented. Thus in our analysis of some of these findings the chain of perceptions can become disconcertingly long, e.g. your perceptions of our perceptions of senior managers' perceptions of the effect of ... etc.

Another concern is the possible desire of respondents to project a particular image of themselves and/or their company, despite our continued emphasis of the confidential nature of the study. It is probable that the responses and open-ended accounts of senior managers are mediated by an in-built PR concern about the image they are conveying. Just as we wished to produce a survey that had managerial credibility and practical utility, so it is likely that many of our respondents sought to convey an image of themselves as 'professional' and 'informed' managers – and similarly, that their organisations were abreast of the latest fashions in management theory. Thus, when answering open-ended questions, many respondents displayed familiarity with the new management jargon using, for example: '*the term we use is empowering the workforce*'; '*it's a very loose-tight thing*'; '*further development of total quality culture*'; '*understanding and practising a new management system founded on profound knowledge*'.

Despite these limitations we believe that our findings are of interest and value. At the very least, they give an indication of how senior managers interpret their world. They also identify the changes that these managers consider most significant and so most likely to influence their actions. For example, both our findings and Wheatley (1992) indicate that total quality management (TQM) is having a substantial impact. It is thus likely that managers will be favourably inclined to support TQM introduction, or its further development within their own organisations. While there is a danger of accepting senior managers' views as the most reliable or important, it is possible to treat them as the voice of one group that contributes to our knowledge and understanding of how management practice has changed.

Whether this voice is shared among other senior and subordinate managers is indicated by the interview data, which widened the respondent sample and so identified contradictions. It is comparatively easy for one senior manager to say that flexibility has increased among all levels of management in his organisation, which in certain respects it may have done, yet his colleague can answer the same question about greater flexibility in this way: *'Definitely not! The opposite. We've become more rigid.... We could actually move quicker than our competition. That has definitely slowed up. There's too many people involved in decision-making now.'*

2.5 The survey evidence

2.5.1 The changing context of management

This examines the background setting or context against which specific changes in management practice within organisations can be analysed and understood. The questions are grouped under three sub-headings:

Changes in the economic context

Six questions were about changes in government economic policies, increased national and international competition, '1992', globalisation of markets and increased efficiency of financial markets.

- Sixty-five per cent perceived the economic context in the UK to be undergoing significant changes. This was consistent with high managerial perceptions of environmental uncertainty, hereafter simply called uncertainty.

- The data suggests that the financial services firms see the extent of change in the UK economic context to be marginally less than that seen by other sectors.
- Firms with higher uncertainty perceive that greater economic changes are taking place.

Changes in the technology context

Measured using five items relating to changes in computer technology, improvements in information systems, changes in work technology, computer-assisted design and computer-aided manufacturing.

- Seventy per cent perceived a highly changing technological context in the UK.
- No important differences were reported between the manufacturing and retailing sectors.
- Firms with higher uncertainty perceived the technology context to be undergoing greater changes, compared with firms with lower uncertainty.

Changes in management ideas

Four items were used as indicators: influence of the Japanese approach, influence of new management gurus, emphasis on flexible management systems, and emphasis on quality.

- Sixty-one per cent said these ideas have been fairly influential in the UK.
- Manufacturing and retailing sectors reported a greater influence of changed management ideas than financial services.
- Firms with higher uncertainty perceive changes in management ideas to be more influential than those with lower uncertainty.

We found the questionnaire responses were consistent. In summary our respondents suggest that their operating contexts, as defined by these three areas, have been undergoing significant changes. As one may expect, firms with higher levels of perceived uncertainty thought these contexts had changed more than firms with lower uncertainty. Manufacturing and retailing firms felt that the influence of management ideas was greater than in financial services, and larger firms thought that the economic context was changing more than smaller firms.

2.5.2 *HRM and levels of management*

This section concerns both the UK corporate sector and internal organisational change initiatives, across all departmental functions and at different management levels. But we limit the discussion to the HRM function and the roles of top, middle and lower management.

The transformation of HRM was assessed by the extent to which management:

- treats its employees as its most important asset;
- has learnt how to manage behavioural change more effectively;
- is investing more heavily in the training and development of staff;
- has recognised the strategic importance of personnel management;
- sees personnel/HRM being more influential in shaping management practice.

The UK corporate sector

- Forty-five per cent of managers perceive that HRM has recently been transformed in the UK, but there is no noticeable difference between manufacturing and retailing and financial services.
- No significant differences were noted between larger or smaller firms.
- Firms with higher uncertainty said UK HRM was undergoing a more substantial transformation than firms with lower uncertainty.

Internal organisational change initiatives

- Respondents broadly agree that changes in the wider national economic context have created a supportive climate, which in turn created a powerful momentum for organisational transformation.
- Firms with confidence in their own ability to negotiate and manage change successfully are more likely to transform their HRM.
- Fifty-one per cent said major transformations were occurring in the HRM function within their own organisations.

The 51 per cent reporting major transformations in their own organisation is somewhat higher than the reported perceptions of HRM transformation in the UK corporate sector as a whole. This could mean:

- a genuine difference, even though fairly small, in the extent of transformation of HRM for our sample compared with the whole UK corporate sector;
- a genuine difference in perceptions of the respondents, which may not be borne out in practice;
- a difference arising from respondents' desire to paint an unrealistic and overdynamic picture of HRM in their organisations.

There was no noticeable difference between manufacturing and retailing and financial services, nor between large and small companies. Firms with higher uncertainty said that HRM was undergoing a more substantial transformation than firms with lower uncertainty, but the difference was very small.

Respondents suggest that there has recently been much greater awareness and appreciation of the importance of HRM, both at the company level and for the UK corporate sector as a whole, these perceptions being greater for higher-uncertainty firms. A possible interpretation is that as firms face more turbulent and hostile environments they see a greater need to develop HRM, both to enhance internal harmony within the workplace and to develop staff so that they can improve their ability to negotiate and manage uncertainty.

We then assessed changes at different levels of management, dividing these into top, middle and lower, by asking respondents to select and rank in order of importance no more than five factors which they considered had fostered change for these levels. They could choose from a list of 24 items.

Panel 1 in Table 2.2 is a summary of the whole sample, ranking the four items seen to be most important. This is self-explanatory, but it is worth noting that:

- the factors relating to both middle and lower management are broadly similar, and mainly internal to the company;
- top management factors were different, mainly external through the national and international economic context.

Table 2.2 Perceptions of transformation of managerial hierarchies, ranked in order of importance

Management Changes in the UK	Level of management: Top	Middle	Lower
1. *Factors fostering change*	International competition National competition Emphasis on quality Economic policy	Emphasis on quality Computer/MIS technology Emphasis on flexibility Improvement in labour relations	Emphasis on quality Computer/MIS technology Improvement in labour relations Changes in work technology
2. *Ways in which work has changed*	More pressure for results More attention to customers Emphasis on short-termism Greater use of computer technology and reliance on quantitative information.	More pressure for results More team work More attention to customers Greater use of computers	More pressure for results More team work More attention to customers Greater use of computers

However, striking differences emerged when the sample was partitioned by industrial sector.

- For top management in the manufacturing and retailing sector, increased international competition and an emphasis on quality were perceived to be the most significant factors.
- In contrast, top managers from financial services perceived increased national competition to be the most important.
- For middle managers the most important factors, quality and computer technology, were similar across both sectors. But in addition, emphasis on flexibility was considered more important in financial services compared with manufacturing and retailing.

No differences were noticeable either for lower management or when classified by degree of perceived uncertainty.

However, when the results were classified by size, the following differences emerged:

- Top managers in smaller companies put a higher priority on quality and see international competition to be less important, compared with those of larger companies.
- Top managers in smaller firms see computer technology to be more important at middle-management level, compared with those in larger firms.
- Top managers in larger firms perceive that greater use of computer technology is more important for lower-level management, compared with those in smaller companies.

To assess the ways in which work has changed, respondents selected and ranked in order of importance no more than five factors which describe the ways in which UK management work has changed during the 1980s. They selected from a list of eighteen items. The lower half of Table 2.2 (see Panel 2) ranks four ways in which work is perceived to have changed for the three managerial levels.

The most striking result is the perception across all three levels of increased:

- pressure for results;
- customer orientation;
- use of computer technology.

In addition, note the emphasis at middle- and lower-management levels on team work.

In summary, our respondents suggest there has recently been a much greater awareness and appreciation of the importance of HRM, at both the individual and corporate-sector level. One interpretation is that this may reflect a perceived need to develop staff and internal harmony using HRM techniques, as a response to a more turbulent and hostile external environment.

In view of the importance of changes in this area we have discussed and analysed the data concerning HRM at much greater length in Chapter 5.

2.5.3 How has change been managed?

Facing significant macro changes in the UK economic, technological and management contexts, respondents have had to develop their own styles to deal with changes at the organisational level. We measured the extent to which management has:

- re-established its prerogative to manage and become more ruthless;
- fostered more positive attitudes to change among the workforce;
- learnt how to manage behavioural and technical change more effectively;
- managed such change more effectively, with minimal resistance.

We sought evidence on the management of change at two levels:

- UK corporate sector: How have other managers managed change?
- Own company: How has his or her own organisation managed change?

Changes in the UK corporate sector

- Seventy-six per cent claim that UK companies have managed change fairly successfully and smoothly, with little resistance from other managerial levels or the workforce.
- Manufacturing and retailing respondents were more positive than financial services. Size had no real impact.
- Firms with higher uncertainty were more positive than those with lower uncertainty.

Changes within own company

- Seventy-four per cent claimed to have managed change fairly successfully and smoothly, with little resistance from other managerial levels or the workforce.
- No important differences between manufacturing and retailing and financial services were reported.
- Larger firms saw themselves to be more successful at managing change than smaller firms.
- Firms with higher uncertainty had marginally higher perceptions of their success than those with lower uncertainty

In summary, respondents perceived that the management of change, both at the UK corporate level and in their own companies, was performed successfully and smoothly. There was little resistance from other managerial levels or the workforce. When compared with those from the financial services sector, respondents from the manufacturing and retailing sector indicated more successful management of change at the level of the UK corporate sector, but not in their own companies. Larger firms perceived themselves to be more successful at managing change, when compared with smaller size firms.

2.6 Discussion

We stress the need for caution and scepticism, since questionnaires are a notoriously 'quick and dirty' method of collecting information. For example, reported variations in responses may be attributable to differences of culture between organisations and sectors, where aspects of change, or strength of view, may be interpreted and expressed differently.

There is also the possibility that respondents are merely recycling progressive ideas about changing management practice, having learnt what is regarded as important or fashionable from management gurus, pundits or academics. There is no way of detecting or controlling this possible reflection of management knowledge. The most we can do is to undertake qualitative research and then compare survey responses with the perceptions of a wider range of employees. If possible this should be complemented with in-depth case studies of organisational change.

Rather than asking respondents a direct question about the changing context of change, therefore, we sought to elicit more specific data: for example, using questions about the importance of the globalisation of markets, the use of computer-aided design and manufacturing, and the influence of Japanese-type approaches to management.

We make the necessary caveat about our dependence upon responses from senior managers. Our results are nevertheless discriminating about the variability of changes across sectors and in relationship to respondents' perceptions of environmental uncertainty. Our evidence suggests that developments in the wider economic context in fact create a favourable climate for change within particular organisations and that there is rapid and continuous change in most large and medium-sized UK companies. The perception that change is widespread has a 'me too' effect, in which senior managers are increasingly receptive to ideas that suggest ways of keeping abreast of such change.

Although we find evidence of increased pressure for results, stronger market or customer orientation and use of technology, there is little to support the more grandiose claims about a sea-change in the management of organisations or the organisation of post-industrial society. Certainly, however, there are strong indications that levels of management are being stripped out, to be replaced by greater horizontal co-ordination of activities through teams and networks. Those retained by their organisations are under increasing pressure to raise their productivity.

Computer technology and total quality management, aimed at avoiding time-consuming efforts to remedy problems, are presented as the means of reducing the pressure for results and productivity. Increased accountability through the formation of business units, combined with performance-related pay, are placing the onus upon individuals to react quickly and to be able to justify their actions. At the same time, the increased emphasis upon team work demands a more collaborative approach to management which can conflict with pressures for increased individual accountability.

2.7 *Summary and conclusions*

We detect significant differences between the financial services sector and manufacturing and retail. Financial services place more emphasis upon the growing importance of national competitiveness, while the latter stress international pressures. Factors fostering change are also perceived to differ between management levels, with those at the top responding more to intensified competition, both national and international.

We identified differences associated with size. Managers in larger organisations tend to emphasise quality less than those in smaller companies, who also gave a stronger emphasis to team work at middle and junior levels of management. Work at these levels is also reported as being changed by the introduction of computer technology. Across all levels, greater pressure for results and productivity is identified as the most significant way in which work has changed, accompanied by a greater attention to the market and customer awareness.

Most managers appear satisfied with the management of change and few report any significant resistance among employees. However, it would appear that change has been less straightforward among financial services companies and in smaller companies, where more reservations were expressed.

We conclude that the changes appear to be of degree, rather than any more radical break with past practice. Our impression is an intensification and individualisation of work, facilitated by new technology and promoted by ideas like TQM. There also appears to be a strong appreciation among senior managers of the key importance of the human resource for managing change. While flexibility is a dominant concept, it seems doubtful that by itself it is adequate to grasp the complexity and diversity of organisational change. 'Speed up' and 'quality management' are perhaps of equal or greater importance as watchwords of contemporary change.

This chapter has reported and analysed evidence drawn from the questionnaire survey. In the next chapter we go on to examine the interview data; in subsequent chapters we link the two phases of the research study.

3
New Organisations and New Managerial Work

3.1 Introduction

Having reported our survey findings in the previous chapter, we now discuss the second phase of the research, which extended the study by establishing extensive qualitative data. We conducted 62 detailed interviews with managers from 20 per cent of the organisations who returned our questionnaire. The sample is defined in Tables 1.2 and 1.3 in Chapter 1. Its balance and representative cross-section depended upon both agreed access and the limitations imposed by our sponsor's research brief, referred to in Chapter 1.

In any future research into the study of changing management practices, we strongly recommend that a greater appreciation of the context of the interviews, including direct observation of management practice, be included. We also recommend that interviews with managers be complemented by attention to other views, not least non-managerial employees, whose conditions of employment and work are being shaped by new wave organisational change.

The data were collected by verbatim tape recording of the interviews, with subsequent transcription and analysis aided by contemporary notes. Interviews were essentially unstructured and open-ended, but we prepared and used a basic schedule as a prompt. This ensured continuity and comparability between different interviewers by highlighting the key research areas, already raised by the questionnaire. We encouraged subjects to speak freely in order to develop those areas that were important to them and which are harder to capture in survey questionnaires, such as the identification of threats they perceived as implicit in the organisational changes they were experiencing.

The data are very extensive, for a one-hour interview can typically generate up to 10,000 words. We can therefore only report the data with a limited number of illustrative quotations, using italics to aid identification in the text. We consciously attempt to be balanced, but recognise that limitations are inevitably imposed by our selection, which could have included many more or different examples. To conclude this introduction we give some typical quotes, taken from an operations manager in a vehicle assembly case study:

> *We latched on to this thing called 'Lean Enterprise' and looked at how we could make our particular enterprise leaner.... We've started launching this thing called 'Group Working' where we've empowered the group.*
>
> *We're putting people from the functions into business units so they don't only perform that one function, they perform others as well. So by putting three men into the business units, you can save four in the functions.*

3.2 Background

The competitive pressures for managers to 'speed up' and 'cut costs', while 'managing quality' and 'delivering results' stimulate organisational change, which Drucker (1988) suggests is a third phase of management development:

> In phase one ownership and control were separated as shareholders appointed a separate cadre of experts to manage their interests. Next the managers introduced bureaucratic techniques and systems to administer the business, culminating in the multidivisional form of large companies. The third and contemporary phase is the shift to an information-based organisation, where managers facilitate and empower.

This shift weakens the traditional reliance on the vertical and horizontal partitioning of organisations into departments and divisions, as cross-functional teams and task forces are developed to tackle problems and exploit opportunities. This demands greater self-discipline and individual responsibility for managing relationships and communications.

> *You'll find a lot of companies, BP and people, are all finding the same problem. They've got a very functional systems environment, which is not conducive to efficient running.* (Director, Manufacturing)

Changing from 'command and control' to 'facilitate and empower' poses a threat to managers who perceive their jobs, status and career opportunities all relying on the traditional second stage mode being perpetuated. According to Drucker, those most threatened by the change are 'the middle-aged people in middle management who tend to be the least mobile'. But it is precisely those occupying the middle layers of management who are expected to implement the new organisation.

Our interview data suggests that middle managers can be used as scapegoats by more senior managers, who got to the top precisely because they are skilled at operating in a command and control world.

> *Middle managers are quite capable of taking on more responsibility. It's the board who don't want to give it away. . . . Right now it's the biggest challenge necessary to implement all this good stuff we're talking about. It has to start in the boardroom.* (Director, Manufacturing)

Where uncertainties and anxieties exist there is an opportunity for experts to help, at a price. Gurus have emerged and multiplied, all advising managers how to meet and beat the challenge by offering solutions like:

- create more flexible forms of organisation;
- strengthen corporate culture and be excellent;
- continuously improve the quality of products and services.

At the heart of many such prescriptions is the recommendation that reliance upon 'hard', rational, mechanical techniques of management and organisation should be moderated by a greater use of 'soft', intuitive, organic methods of management.

> What our [7S] framework has really done is to remind the world of professional managers that 'soft is hard'. It has enabled us to say, in effect, All that stuff you have been dismissing for so long as the intractable, irrational, intuitive, informal organisation *can* be managed. (Peters and Waterman, 1982)

Managers are rightly sceptical of the guru exhortations. They see weaknesses, especially those which threaten their security and career. But the pressure to be proactive and survive in a hostile market makes them vulnerable to expert advice – from consultants, for example, who often recycle these ideas. Or they may flirt with the ideas of new management theory, in an effort to adapt themselves or their organisations to rapidly changing and unpredictable conditions.

Many publications seek to teach and reassure managers that strategic change can be successfully managed by adopting the latest recipe. Little research examines the associated practical difficulties, however, not least because managers and consultants are reluctant to publicly admit failure, even though this would be instructive to others. We therefore only read the 'success' stories. Our research tries to illuminate this shadowy area of change implementation, as managers wrestle with a series of conundrums that the pundits (perhaps conveniently) overlook. Quick-fix solutions often pay minimal attention to implementation.

We recommend that such limitations are given greater attention to better orient managers for the new realities and encourage more questioning attitudes. This would support increasing self-confidence and expand competencies, while reducing dependence upon the simplistic ideas peddled by the gurus.

3.3 *New wave management*

New wave management questions received wisdom about how to effectively organise and manage. Organisations should be leaner, more creative and adaptive. Bureaucracy and hierarchical control are particularly criticised, as departmental divisions and layers of management are said to:

- inhibit effective communication;
- create unnecessary overheads;
- limit the speed and quality of responses to changing conditions;
- impose deadening effects upon employee initiative and productivity;
- mechanically rely upon rules and procedures.

Instead, it is said that the new organisation will be a network, with a shared culture. Once employees are committed to the core values of the organisation, so the cumbersome hierarchy (and its cost) can be minimised. Shared values, rather than inflexible and outdated regulations, guide and control employees, and suggested changes are summarised in Table 3.1.

Table 3.1 Projected developments in new wave management

The past relied upon:	Future emphasis will be to:
Rules, regulation and supervision e.g., a span of control	Flexibly appreciate contingency and ambiguity
Hierarchical control and a clear chain of command	Effectively develop human resources
Discipline imposed by management	Facilitate employee self-discipline
A mechanistic and directive approach to problem-solving	Problem-solve through participation
Single-function specialists and individualism or independence	Create multi-functional teams through mutual dependence
Job descriptions with defined tasks and responsibilities	Continuously review a fluid series of renegotiated assignments

In this new form of organisation managers are no longer required to develop and enforce rules to control the workforce. Employees will be self-disciplined and no longer require a narrow span of control to ensure compliance, and thus hierarchical levels can be reduced, if not abandoned. The remaining managers act as facilitators, who ensure that the staff are fully trained and properly equipped, which requires new forms of management. A reliance upon hierarchical position is supplanted by an ability to create and encourage interdepartmental and cross-functional collaborative activity.

Functional specialisms and boundaries are seen as obstacles to the close co-operation and mutual understanding needed for effective project management and innovation. Associated with these developments is a view of staff as customers of each other's services. This leads to an emphasis upon the level and quality of service provided by a manager to his or her staff. There is also a trend to measure and evaluate such services in terms of the value-added provided by management specialists.

Command is replaced by consent. Corporate success relies upon employees operating with minimal direction. Following the rules and watching one's back is no longer a low-risk strategy for achieving recognition and promotion. Advancement depends upon demonstrating skills that empower, energise and support staff. Such increasingly interdependent relationships mean individual managers have to get results from staff where there may be no formal reporting relationship. A key issue is the manager's interpersonal and political skills in building and using strategic alliances to form relevant networks.

> In the emerging organisation, managers add value by deal-making, by brokering at interfaces, rather than by presiding over their individual empires.... Executives must be able to juggle a set of constituencies rather than control a set of subordinates. They have to bargain, negotiate, and sell instead of making unilateral decisions and issuing commands. (Kanter, 1989)

This is a potentially bewildering world. The old certainties associated with the prerogative of rank and the authority of expertise no longer provide a reliable basis for action. In the effort to eliminate rigidities and improve responsiveness it seems that almost everything will become flexible and negotiable. Managers will be valued for their contribution in unsettling those conventions and rigidities that are deemed to be counterproductive for stimulating innovation and enhancing competitiveness. Managers and employees are no longer urged to strive for excellence. Instead, they are exhorted to 'cherish impermanence' and 'thrive on chaos' (Peters, 1989).

3.4 The practicalities of change

Our interviewees expressed a widespread view that major shifts were occurring in their environment and that survival depended upon developing 'a different approach' to managing people and change. In manufacturing, the intensification of international competition was frequently said to be the main reason for change. Japanese methods had to be copied or beaten, while recognising that these needed adaptation for the UK culture: *'the big thing was competitive pressure, particularly from the Japanese, and that meant we had to look at different ways of doing business and a different approach'.*

(Finance Director, Manufacturing)

A Director of Quality said his company was seeking to *'put in a culture that's very similar to the Japanese'*, but it would include profit centres intended to *'release the entrepreneurial spirit'* of individual employees. This would compensate for the relative lack of team discipline in UK workers by exploiting their individualism. This director also admitted his uncertainty about the practicality of this policy: *'Now how you pull that off, I don't know.'*

Financial services were not so preoccupied with international competition, being more concerned with domestic companies that *'haven't got the fat on them'*. In this sector the use of financial and management information by competitors led to a productivity and effectiveness programme in response. The installation of a *'fundamentally very simple work measurement system'* was said to *'empower'* managers by requiring them to quantify the contribution of their staff against planned improvements in performance. It seems the terminology, or rhetoric, of new management theory is being used to describe a typical case of command and control, a bureaucratic system introduced to direct effort while measuring and raising productivity.

Evidence shows that the idea of empowerment creates anxiety in managers, so it is perhaps not surprising that it is used to justify tighter management control.

> *I have no problem with the idea of empowerment, it's just the practical application I'm worried about. I don't mind empowering people so long as we actually train them to get a better answer before they're let loose.* *(Customer Services Manager, Financial Services)*

This quote draws attention to the complex conditions and consequences of implementing the new organisation. Empowering employees is all very well as long as they act in ways that are acceptable to management, a concern that becomes more critical as managerial rewards are linked to staff performance. Our interviewees generally accepted the need to change and develop a new organisational approach, but feared that pushing for empowerment and commitment might damage established qualities of pride and loyalty without replacing them with more effective and robust alternatives.

A major difficulty is that the new organisation works as a total package, and transforming from command and control to facilitate and empower cannot happen overnight. It is a 'chicken and egg' situation, since ideally all parts of the organisation need to be changed simultaneously, but in practice managers must start somewhere. Because command and control cultures are familiar with structural change, many of our case studies started this way. However, it was then either recognised or discovered that other issues had to be tackled first, but this was difficult without changing the structure.

> *You can't just tackle structure on its own because if you change that and not other key issues, then you'll fall over. We did something about culture, but then there's personnel, you need new pay and performance appraisal systems, you have to change all those as well.*
> *(Employee Relations Director, Manufacturing)*

Many companies are struggling to change systems and human resource management in an effort to create the new organisation. At the same time, however, while lip service is paid to the new management ideas, many contradictory and established values and practices are often retained in whole or part, such as:

- functional specialisms are guarded;
- hierarchical position continues to be a power base;
- established political allegiances are preserved.

We found that command and control often lives on beneath the shining surface of the new organisation. There seem to be two major reasons for this.

The first is practical. It is simply too difficult to change everything at once.

The second reason is political. At first such change is painful and resisted, because it increases uncertainty and insecurity. Until the new methods are fully installed and taken for granted, there is a sense of loss before there is any equivalent sense of gain. Moreover, the loss is often accompanied by disillusionment, as expectations are not fulfilled. An increased attention to accountability was another strong theme of our interviews, as employees' notions of increased independence and freedom are reversed.

> *We're trying to get away from rigid structures, but you can't just give everybody* carte blanche *to do their own thing. So I mean you must have some boundary conditions again. The empowerment has to go with some accountability. You've got to accept the accountability.*
> *(Finance Director, Manufacturing)*

We found that moves to the new organisation were often associated with increased anxiety. Thus it was that arguments to justify the *status quo*, which used new management language, revealed a wish to retain the regularities and certainty of the old organisation. While people may *'enjoy having a bit more control over their own destiny and their own day-to-day roles and responsibilities' (Finance Director, Manufacturing)*, they seem even keener to maintain control over the destiny, roles and responsibilities of others.

Many managers, including the most senior, continue to see preserving this command and control basis of their authority as the main way of protecting the relative freedom they have enjoyed in the past. It is for this reason that management practices which support and sustain this system are proving difficult to change. Another of our interviewees correctly diagnosed the problem: *'People who don't want to work that way take some time to convince and it's management's willingness to let go that matters.'*

3.5 *Interpreting the evidence*

One way to explain away our evidence is by using the label 'teething troubles', implying a natural inevitability that such problems always accompany changes in established routines. But this interpretation overlooks important differences between technical and social processes. While the former might be driven by impersonal forces, the latter are politically negotiated as different groups persuade or coerce others to preserve their privileges. In so far as teething troubles exist, they are as much a product of politics as they are the outcome of technical difficulties in achieving change.

Another explanation may accept that managing change is political, but ascribes any difficulties to a lack of knowledge about how to manage change successfully. It also assumes that the division between managers and managed is functional, maintaining this view even when, as in the new organisation, these divisions are simultaneously regarded as a major source of ineffectiveness. From this perspective, difficulties encountered in implementing the new organisation are put down to the inadequate understanding and/or education of managers.

Peters and Waterman, for example, presented a few companies as examples of 'excellence', thus implicitly castigating the vast majority of managers who do not exhibit attributes like 'bias for action' and 'hands on, value driven'. However, within a few years many of his examples (such as IBM) had declined, so Peters revised his message. Pursuing the attributes of excellence is no longer the mark of a competent manager because 'Excellent firms don't believe in excellence – only in constant improvement and change' (Peters, 1989).

Similarly, Pascale says that managers are 'gimmick junkies', constantly moving from one fad to another, in search of an elixir. He thus now urges managers to rely more on their own experience and intuition, and to learn from failures and disappointments. Failure to create the new organisation is due to the defective mindset or attitudes of managers. This can be corrected by copying managers at Honda, who embody the 'magic' of the new organisation (Pascale, 1991). If only change were so easy, and the politics of change were so uncontentious!

We agree there is considerable scope for managers to shift their attitudes, but it is potentially misleading to imply that the difficulties of management arise exclusively, or even predominantly, from a lack of relevant education or a deluded attitude. It is misleading because this interpretation takes little or no account of the historical and institutional context or the politics of management. Like many gurus, Pascale assumes the practical difficulties encountered in creating the new organisation can be overcome by adopting a favoured recipe. In his case this takes the form of a mindset that effectively juggles contradictory demands of consistency and continuity with diversity and innovation.

This view represents conflict as a functional feature of organisational life, as long as it is managed effectively. What it overlooks is the dependence of managers upon other employees and the associated difficulty of making them accept, and be committed to, the solutions generated by this new set of values or attitudes. In the Japanese context this may be comparatively effortless and uncomplicated, because employees are culturally trained to respect authority and be unquestioningly loyal to their employer. But, as our interviewees noted, we have a different culture. Individualism and freedom are prized, while unquestioning respect for authority is in short supply. At best managers might hope to achieve either compliant conformity or, alternatively, a selective and instrumental commitment to corporate objectives.

In this respect our interviewees often demonstrated a keener sense of the realities of implementing the new organisation than the pundits who are urging its development: *'Although I've always seen the sense in restructuring, I think going from a total functional company, that was not working well, to a total line was too much of a jump.*
(Financial Controller, Extractive)

Of course, some managers were at an early stage on the learning curve, struggling to grasp the nature and scope of the changes. Many others had got to the point of accepting the need for major change, but were using the new management language of networking, empowerment, quality-driven, and the like, to describe quite conventional management programmes. There was often a conscious acknowledgement of how the appeal of concepts like empowerment was being used to induce and justify command and control type changes: *'We've introduced multiskilling which is, it seems to me from a cynical point of view, more training people who are trained as electricians, or whatever, to learn how to paint.' (Financial Controller, Manufacturing)*

In general there was a reluctance to dilute or weaken hierarchical control. Sometimes this took the form of outright rejection of the new management methods as impractical and 'airy-fairy'. More often these methods were used highly selectively and the language adopted to push change that was only a small incremental move to 'facilitate-and-empower'. In this way managers could appear as progressive, while simultaneously preserving a command and control structure. They favour an approach that could be described either as 'sensible and cautious' or 'cynical and self-serving', but which was justified in terms of the need to retain control, in the form of accountability:

> *I think making people accountable and spreading decision-making around in a controlled manner is good for the company. But some*

> *people have struggled because they thought they were getting independence but find that they don't have that decision-making freedom.* (*Financial Controller, Extractive*)

Our interviewees recognised and understood a basic conflict of interest better than the pundits. Employees, conditioned by the values of individualism, would prefer carte blanche to do their own thing, but senior managers are accountable to shareholders for profitable growth. In the Japanese context there is a cultural tradition, and a national industrial strategy, of supporting lifetime employment in the major companies, so developing employee loyalty and commitment is relatively easy. At the same time, accountability comes through a combination of the individual's material dependence upon the employer and the confirmation of identity that follows from belonging to the company.

In contrast, Western employees are induced to work by market forces, so those with scarce skills can make greater demands upon the employer. Common ground is found by linking improved job security and career advancement with productivity and added value. But this foundation is fragile and the contradiction of appealing to individualism to increase collective effort was signalled by a number of our interviewees.

> *If you really want to move to a remuneration system that says, 'Look, I only succeed if the company succeeds', you want to go to a salesman and tell him that you'll pay him if the company succeeds, not if he gets orders.* (*Systems and Quality Director, Manufacturing*)

Perhaps sales staff are exceptionally concerned with individual performance and reward.

The idea that reward should be linked to collective performance, over which individual employees have little influence, rather than individual contribution is unlikely to find much support among employees conditioned by a culture of individualism. A response to this obstacle, which is strongly favoured by a number of the gurus, is to 'change the culture'. However, given that assumptions of individualism are deeply embedded, then enthusiasm for cultural change may be limited, unless aided by individual inducement and so perpetuating established individualism.

In some companies, employees are encouraged to see career

advancement less in terms of movement up the ladder than as skills development through movement sideways, or even downwards. But even where recession limits career opportunities within and between companies, such efforts to redefine career development do not seem to be greeted with enthusiasm. As an interviewee said: '*With the increase in teamwork, we see the future more as development through jobs... but it's very difficult.*' However, once the cyclical economic climate changes yet again, we suggest that minimal espoused compliance with such changes may well mutate into more overt resistance.

We believe that managers are right to be sceptical and cautious about the claims that are made for the new organisation and the new managerial work. It is a basic fallacy to assume that, in a capitalist economy, a coincidence of interest between employers and employees can be contrived through the adoption of a different philosophy or mindset of attitudes. As an interviewee noted, '*you can't replicate the Japanese culturally*'. We strongly agree with this quote, for it is foolhardy to believe that practices that work well in Japan can automatically and simply be transplanted into the West.

3.6 Conclusions

We have found strong evidence suggesting that managers know about the new management and have a commitment to it. At the same time, many showed a keener understanding of its limitations and difficulties than is acknowledged by its leading proponents. In part this can be explained in terms of managers' resistance to abandon or dilute established structures and values that secure their position of authority. While such an explanation is valid, it is also insufficient.

It is also important to connect managers' scepticism and resistance to the new management to a keen grasp of its limited practicality, for its introduction may jeopardise and undermine the co-operation and trust generated by the very predictability and coherence of the command and control approach. Under this structure responsibilities are clearly demarcated and the requirement to be innovative, proactive and collaborative is minimal. But more importantly the new organisation may be fundamentally in conflict with the employee's cultural values.

We suggest that, at best, cultural change programmes can hope to induce employees to manage the appearance of operating a facilitate-and-empower philosophy, but only if this is calculated by the individual employee to increase his or her job security, job satisfaction or career prospects. At worst, implementation of the new organisation, without regard for the contradiction between corporate demands and employee values, is likely to produce incoherence, confusion and resistance. In this case, even with the best-laid plans supported by generous resources, it will come to grief in the form of widespread demoralisation and cynicism.

As the experience of many of our interviewees has shown, translating the ideals of the new management theory into practical realities is not just difficult, but potentially counter-productive. For those concerned with the performance of UK companies there are clearly grounds for disquiet about a minority of companies where the adoption of the new management theory is uncritical and therefore obsessive. This concern should also, perhaps, be extended to companies where scepticism has yet to produce a sustained and articulate diagnosis and critique of the limitations of new managerial work and new organisations.

We have now reported some of the interview data and in the next chapters use all the data from this study to focus on particular areas of change. In Chapter 4 the specific focus is flexibility, as achieved through delayering and multiskilling.

4 Delayering and Multiskilling

4.1 Introduction

Delayering, which is defined below, and multiskilling are key elements of organisational transformation and major issues for our research. They are prescribed as essential steps to achieve necessary flexibility, but their imposition does not exclusively, or even predominantly, affect just shop-floor workers. In this chapter we suggest that these changes can be seen either as methods of crude control and cost reduction, or presented and masked by a seductive language of employee empowerment and freedom. Despite the hype, our evidence indicates no real shift from direct control to self-discipline and autonomy, nor even their parallel existence.

Using interview evidence and a case study, we analyse and criticise new wave management philosophy to highlight its deficiencies and contradictions. We show that external factors limit the possibility of employee resistance, and how senior management can more ruthlessly exert greater control over compliant staff, at all levels. This suggests that the prerogative to manage, thought to have been undermined in the 1960s and 1970s, is as strong as it ever was.

Management style is influenced by a need for short-term success in controlling costs and demonstrating results. Multiskilled employees are empowered if – and only if – they make the right decisions, as tested and measured by profits. We suggest that it is wrong to assume that new wave remedies remove political obstacles to progress, or that these blocks result from an incompetent or partial implementation of the prescription.

Rather, we conclude that such obstacles are an inevitable part of the proposed new organisation, but are largely ignored by the theory and practice of new wave management, which we first examine.

4.2 *Background*

To compete successfully in a global market-place, management writers stress that organisations must improve flexibility, strengthen culture and raise quality standards. Japanese and Pacific Rim companies are held up as models of good modern practice, and to survive (let alone prosper) managements are told to become leaner and more market responsive. Organisations must be more adaptable, so their managers must prepare for and accept rapid change. To achieve this transformation it is necessary to delayer, which means:

- becoming market-driven and closer to the customer;
- removing what are now seen as redundant levels of the management hierarchy;
- promoting and implementing multiskilling throughout the organisation;
- using new technologies to improve the speed and quality of all their activities.

The background and context of this new wave management thinking has been described earlier, and is not now repeated. Rather, we focus on the evidence relating to delayering and multiskilling as examples of changes that are reshaping UK organisations. A case study of a vehicle assembly plant is used to reveal the dynamics and unintended consequences of these changes. In this we explore more fully some of the unacknowledged tensions and problems that underlie solutions derived from new management thinking.

4.3 *The new wave prescription*

The new wave approach to management attacks the unresponsiveness and inflexibility of companies, which is said to result from a bureaucratic mentality. This mentality places an excessive reliance upon mechanistic rules and procedures, with hierarchical divisions between managers and workers. Employee involvement in quality and productivity improvement is inhibited, while the domination of a hard-nosed rational approach to decision-making is encouraged.

Peters (1989) advocates a shift from extended hierarchies to flatter structures, breaking down functional barriers. Middle managers are re-labelled 'horizontal managers' and become facilitators rather than supervisors, or 'turf guardians'.

Similarly, Waterman (1988) champions the destruction of barriers, the promotion of transforming leaders at all levels, and the building of networks to facilitate team work. Rigid procedures should be decentralised and replaced by flexible interactive systems. These will enhance the speed and relevance of decisions and communications, both within companies and with suppliers and customers. So middle managers are expected to be held responsible for 'battering down the very functional barriers they were formerly paid to protect'. (Peters, 1989)

It is not difficult to make a connection between delayering and multiskilling on the one hand, and increased flexibility through reduced bureaucracy on the other. Overlayered structures may be perceived to promote meticulous and detailed control over all elements of work. They carry high costs and their rigidity inhibits initiative, experimentation and flexibility. Firms with overlayered structures are said to be ill equipped to act decisively and respond to hostile competition and rapidly changing technology.

Having expressed concerns about the diagnoses and solutions offered by the gurus, we now summarise empirical evidence to support our conclusions and recommendations. We quote typical responses, as recorded in interviews, which capture the views of managers directly involved with change processes. We examine the drivers for delayering and multiskilling they identified and the extent to which new wave prescriptions are being implemented. Finally, we consider the dynamics and processes of change through the case study.

4.4 *The drive to delayer*

Motivated to cut costs, interviewees claim great success with extensive delayering programmes to reduce headcount. They cite increased employee involvement, regular communication and good redundancy schemes as key actions in achieving that success. The evidence also shows how possible resistance to such major change has been lessened by the economic recession and a much weakened trade union movement. Many firms said their hierarchical structures have been significantly changed to produce flatter and leaner organisations, with delayering at all managerial levels. But the evidence suggests that most casualties are from middle management, with many interviewees claiming a simplified managerial structure of only three levels, the following example being typical of many similar comments: '*We used to have seven or eight conceptual layers. In the new organisation there are three layers.*' *(Quality and Systems Director, Electronics Manufacturer)*

In many companies, the quest for delayering appears to have accompanied a drive for the creation of business units, replacing a strict functional hierarchy:

> *We essentially divided into two strategic business units. I took the second level players that I thought were capable and gave them a lot more scope and power. We took the design group and put them in with production control, purchasing, industrial engineering and an element of sales. The idea was that the whole was greater than the sum of the parts.*
> *(Manufacturing Director, Engineering)*

Two associated forms of delayering seem to be taking place:

- shifting existing staff to new functions/units with new roles;
- staff reductions, sometimes up to 40–50 per cent.

Such statistics conceal larger reductions in specific locations and functions:

> *In the early 80s we had about 100 in accounts payable. I looked at [a company in Japan of a similar size] and found that they had only two, which gave us some ideas. So I'm down to just over 20, but not yet down to two. And you can say the same right across the factory floor.*
> *(Finance Director, Motor Manufacturer)*

The drive to delayer is associated with two justifications: economic efficiency and speed of communication. These echo the management gurus. Claims like '*We doubled revenue without increasing the number of people*' were common, as were reports that bureaucracy was reduced after delayering: '*We weren't so much aiming to take out*

hierarchy as to take out bureaucracy, as we wanted people to do things, rather than check if someone else was doing what they should be doing.'
(Managing Director, Manufacturing)

4.4.1 The economic context of delayering

Virtually every interviewee said the economic environment had been extremely turbulent and hostile, *'the toughest I have known in over 30 years'*. To survive in recession required significant savings in labour costs, by avoiding duplication and intensifying work by expanding jobs. New technology provided more scope for savings, possibly by imitating competitors, for example: *'no invoices, they paid by ERS, automatically crediting deliveries via the interbank computer bureau. So we did that.' (Finance Director, Motor Manufacturer)*

The recession was also seen as an opportunity for managers to exercise their prerogative and implement initiatives that would have been less acceptable in a prosperous economic climate. Managers themselves were seen to be the main casualties of such change:

> *Businesses look at their management structures and say, 'Do we need this management structure?' A lot of it is self-perpetuating. So you take levels of management out along with big costs because they've got cars and BUPA, etc. You still take out the odd shop-floor one, but they haven't suffered as much as white-collar and middle management.*
> *(Finance Director, Electronics)*

The opportunity afforded by the recession was used by management to make swift and radical reductions in personnel and in management layers, as it was felt the workforce was less resistant to change. Most interviewees presumed the effects of the recession were so obvious that most of those adversely affected would see the outcome as inevitable. The reasons were 'outside economic forces', and so management was not to blame.

It is worth noting the contradiction between attributing job losses to outside forces and the key role that new wave managers claim in achieving success. The distinctive external factors in Japan are largely ignored, but the UK recessionary context is nevertheless seen to both require and facilitate the introduction of a new Japanese-style management.

4.4.2 Communication, persuasion and resistance

Interviewees suggest that frequent communications between top management and the workforce had helped to reduce resistance to job losses.

> *Nobody in our organisation can say they don't understand what needs to be done, we have shared with them all the bad news and all the good news. In fact, its easier to share the bad news.*
>
> *(Head of Human Resources, Manufacturing)*

The success of these communication exercises were taken as evidence of a greater realism on the part of the workforce: *'I think while people may not always agree with what's going on, they do understand why it's happening.' (National Sales Manager, Agro-chemicals)*

The sources of consensus between senior managers and the shop floor were seen as communication, training and, externally, the market and economy.

> *We said, 'Pretend you're the board. What are our priorities?' Three teams came back and said, 'We've got to cut waste and develop new products,' and other logical things. It was all very sensible.*
>
> *(Finance and Strategy Director, Steel)*

What motivated these teams to come up with these solutions is not clear. They may reflect employees' genuine perceptions of the problem. They may be due to success in training shop-floor workers to think in management terms. Or they may have been suggested because shop-floor workers had little option but to say what management wanted to hear. Irrespective of the motivation, however, these sensible and logical solutions are used by management as evidence of the way shop-floor workers think and of their attitudes.

Very limited opportunities to resist change were seen. Indeed, competition for a job, never mind promotion, was an incentive to advance ideas that could result in peer group and, ultimately, self-redundancy.

> *It's better to represent your role as surplus in a controlled way; if you don't roll along with it you and all the company might go for a wrong rather than a good reason. So there's a certain logic to it.*
> *(Personnel Manager, Automotive Parts)*

Job losses affected not only those made redundant. The survivors carried a heavier workload and increased sense of responsibility. The perceived professionalism of managers was seen as an important reason why this extra work was accepted. Others preferred to play a waiting game of temporary co-operation, intending to secure another job when the time was right. New wave management thus polarises the staff, and those who are not part of the solution are seen as part of the problem.

> *Essentially, most of them have said, 'OK, this is my lot, but how can I improve it?' It's been an incentive to some but others just switched off. One or two have said, 'OK, I'm just going to tread water until things get better and then move on'. So we cover for those skills when they do decide to go; by doing more cross-functional training we're covering all the time.* *(Finance Director, Electronics)*

Effective communication, across all management levels, was seen as an important means of securing the co-operation and compliance of employees. Managers bluntly described how employee resistance to imposed changes and job losses was constrained by record unemployment and poor job mobility. Such pessimism was also reinforced by weakened trade unions: *'The present recession helps in the sense that it's very cold out on the street, right?' (Finance Director, Motor Manufacturer)*

However, it is easy to overlook that, in addition to staff reductions by delayering, usually below the top management level, there is a consequent and necessary redefinition of roles and responsibilities for those remaining. In most companies a problem after delayering was how to readjust previously taken-for-granted assumptions coupled with habitual ways of thinking and operating. This was needed to cope with the new structure:

> *In the past managers' prestige and pay was closely linked to their headcount. Now, if you denude those traditional measures you hit his perceived importance as well. Cross-functional teams require people to set aside these concerns, as their contribution is as big, as long as they interact and share knowledge and experience so that the team is more successful.* *(Plant Manager, Engineering)*

We suggest that too little attention is drawn to such problems when simplistic prescriptive solutions are offered, like delayering consequent upon business process re-engineering (BPR).

4.5 The drive to multiskill and team work

Most interviewees said multiskilling and associated flexibility was a significant change, appearing to take two forms: broadening technical skills and improving the ability of personnel to work in teams. We also find that some companies have equated the inconsistency of multiskilling and team working with a high level of functional specialism. While the problems of encouraging individual initiative within a team are recognised, they are not yet fully addressed.

Operators, supervisors, and technicians are expected to do more tasks, and troubleshoot, across much larger areas. Alongside these developments is a drive to increase control over the labour force, but this may be dressed up as team working or job enrichment and employee empowerment. Sometimes there was an acknowledgement of how the appeal of a concept like empowerment was being used to induce and justify changes of a command and control type.

> *We took all the people who have been doing bits of jobs and sat them in the same room to start with and then we trained them to do the other bits they didn't know how to do.*
>
> *(Assistant General Manager, Financial Services)*

Many interviewees said obvious company benefits come from increased flexibility. Multiskilling enables staff to be shifted to different and multiple tasks, depending on demand. Labour utilisation is increased, costs are reduced and sales response enhanced, a typical quote being:

> *Now a maintenance technician can grab a fitter and say, 'You pull this pump out, I'll go and get the bits, you do the basic work'. We expect operators to be flexible in assisting maintenance or colleagues. Because we've gradually given them bigger and bigger areas so if one guy hastrouble in his area we expect another guy to go and assist him there.*
>
> *(Operations Manager, Agro-chemicals)*

Staff development policies resulted from the need to manage in new ways. Focusing on training for multiskilling, they could also be promoted as career development, and were aided by carefully designed voluntary redundancy schemes which targeted those deemed less attractive to the new organisation. The remaining staff were then more suitable material for multiskilling.

4.5.1 *Flexing management muscles*

We have suggested that new wave thinking divides managers into solutions and problems. Voluntary redundancy offers a solution for recalcitrant managers, since age and length of service were seen to correlate strongly with a lack of flexibility, and technical expertise was little help with unwillingness to change:

> *Some are never going to change, we have to accept that fact and manage it. My view is we identify those we want to leave and make it as uncomfortable as possible and not be ambiguous. Selected people have been invited to leave as well, those whose views are not consistent with the board's direction have gone. We need to accelerate that process.*
> *(Human Resource Manager, Financial Services)*

Even when delayering and multiskilling are successfully introduced, they can have unintended consequences for managerial effectiveness:

> *A great strength was our speed at moving, it gave us an edge over competitors, but that's definitely slowed up, the changes made it worse. There's too many people involved in decisions now. Nobody knows what decisions they can make. It goes through an asset manager, then a business unit manager and then to the executive anyway. Whereas in the past it would've gone straight to the executive, so we've just built in many more loops.*
> *(Financial Controller, Oil)*

Paradoxically, delayering can be accompanied by the involvement of more staff in decision-making and by a more cumbersome lateral sequence of steps in a networked hierarchy. This danger is not often pointed out by the gurus, but it is a key point that practitioners should bear in mind when planning a reorganisation.

4.5.2 *More control or less?*

Superficially, multiskilling initiatives may appear to be key elements of carefully thought out programmes of job enlargement and enrichment, which seek to make tasks more appealing and satisfying. Many interviewees see the drive to multiskill leading to an increased emphasis on team work and coinciding with a reduced emphasis on bureaucracy, while some managers see team work as being empowerment and increased communication:

> *We've started 'Group Working' where we've empowered the group. We've increased communication with the workforce by something like five- or tenfold, and managers are more proactive.*
> *(Operations Manager, Vehicle Assembly)*

However, other managers expressed concern about the reduction of managerial control that team work caused. The importance of hierarchy and centralised direction of activities were emphasised, for if teams were occupied with immediate tasks, then other managerial levels needed to plan strategically:

> *A team highly focused on a task may not be as effective as some think in doing traditional management functions of looking a year ahead to see opportunities emerging and getting ready for them. So don't we still need a level to do that strategic planning, if you will? But by all means use teams in a cross-functional way to take care of normal business functions.* *(Plant Manager, Engineering)*

This manager highlights how the necessary co-ordination and overview is provided by a traditional hierarchy. Even if this is delayered or dismantled, the need for supervisory control still remains, so the manager was expressing concerns about the weakening of disciplinary power that team work could cause:

> *Peer pressure may keep a team up to scratch. But it can move to the lowest common denominator because the other side of peer pressure is that everybody just wants to get along. So you still need some review or control process.*

Just as we found with delayering, in some companies multiskilling and team work also pose a paradox, for in seeking to develop team spirit individual initiative may be undermined. Once again, we suggest that too little attention is drawn to such side effects as the expert writes out the patient's prescription.

4.6 The dynamics of change – a case study

By focusing upon a single case, we are able to explore and demonstrate in much greater depth the way managers handle change. We are grateful to the managers of a vehicle assembly plant for their patience in providing data from which this case study was created.

We suggest that this example is typical of the general moves to delayering and multiskilling in the pursuit of reduced costs, increased flexibility and more intensified management control.

Threats and opportunities

This company adopted new wave management in response to increasing Japanese competition, the recession and guru encouragement. As in many other companies the need for change was very evident, but the appropriate solutions were not so apparent. Consider this comment on timing and context as, like many others, competition is a rationale to reduce labour costs:

> *In 1986, a few of us who'd seen Peters, etc., pushed for change, but the climate wasn't right, no one listened. The merger helped, we got into Europe fast, it's very competitive. We've used the economic crisis and recession, etc. Nothing wrong with crisis, it's helped us do a lot, get people on side, particularly unions. We've kept pushing, lots of communication.* *(Employee Relations Director)*

Even though other reasons were given for large redundancies, a few less-guarded statements reveal a deep-seated ambition to reduce costs:

> *And being slightly cynical I suspect most companies delayer largely because they just want the costs down.*
> *(Training and Development Manager)*

Involvement and empowerment

Radical reductions in management, combined with a new structure, had other, perhaps unexpected, effects which then drove more changes, necessitating other new ways of working and managing. One result is a wider involvement in decision-making:

> *Delayering forces us to allow them to participate. Instead of 500 people making decisions and the others assembling, we now have 5,500 all involved in making the business better and its decisions.*
>
> *(Training and Development Manager)*

Participation and involvement were intended to be a break with tradition, a general acceptance of the new way of managing. Employees and managers alike were to participate in reconstructing the organisation. All would realise the advantages of behaving appropriately and, by participating, management assumed employees would become *'a lot more prepared to contribute to the business'*. But senior management could not say the wrong or unacceptable things, at least not with any realistic expectation of a successful outcome.

Although managers did admit the context of their change agenda, they were able to represent this as a drive for flexibility. The route was mapped out with guru rationality, to be dressed up and presented as a more democratic style:

> *If you try and impose the flexibility without the people working together, it's very difficult. So what you do is you get them working together in groups and that in itself makes them more flexible. That's us relinquishing some control as well, so there is a price to pay.*
>
> *(Operations Manager)*

The secret of success was seen to be a matter of using the right management style, and so releasing the workforce potential to deliver a commercial advantage: *'Empowerment, I suppose, really is the key word.'*

Cultural control and peer pressure

The seductive new management style of employee empowerment aims to achieve precisely the same as the top-down command and control mode:

> *Half the supervisors got a much broader role under the production manager as they direct the workforce much less because they are now more self-disciplined so you expect them to accept control by themselves.*
>
> *(Operations Manager)*

This raises questions about the apparently limited resistance by staff negatively affected by these changes.

- Are employees so seduced by this more subtle management style that they fail to appreciate the consequences for themselves?
- Is management becoming more successful at making employees think and act as they wish them to?
- Do employees find the new management style quite transparent, but that other forces prevent resistance?
- Are employees' attitudes to change initiatives independent of management style, and do they instead indicate some self-sacrifice to benefit future generations?

Our interviews shed light on a number of these issues, the reactions by shop-floor staff and middle managers to the changes, which were apparently accepted with virtually no resistance. A consensus, it was claimed, was secured by various means, for example training and increased communication:

> *When restructuring we had outsiders interview everyone, almost a subordinate appraisal. Not surprisingly, the top concern was job security. But next was the amount involvement was mentioned. People are not getting involved, and they want to, so we're missing an opportunity here.* (Employee Relations Director)

> *We started with a quality awareness education package and now we've almost got the quality ethic into the fabric of the building.* (Operations Manager)

Those not toeing the corporate line were likened to extremes in a statistical distribution, that can be truncated at will to achieve a normal distribution. It was claimed that direction is not the answer, but rather cultural control through peer pressure. In looking closely at attendance, for example, they considered removing the time clock. Instead of punishment or supervisory sanctions, they intended to rely on peer pressure from the new team ethic in order to ensure good timekeeping and reduce unnecessary absence.

Regulation by communication and training

The emphasis by top management on regulating practices and getting peer group controlled obedience was evident in how individuals were managed. One area was increased communication with subordinates:

> *We need to communicate and be much more open than before, so we lose a lot of the traditional controls. You can no longer shout 'Shit!' and*

> *expect them to jump on a shovel, they won't. But when you do agree to something, it is jointly and so it goes through more easily. We've made changes recently much more quickly than before. Without the communication, without the involvement, it would've taken us two or three times as long.* *(Operations Manager)*

Regular communication is used to smooth change, to monitor past performance and to plan future action. It is also used to improve motivation by creating either space for individuals to express themselves, or the myth of a democratic environment. Communication is a way of training subordinates to see the world in the same way as managers. Recalcitrant managers were warned of the personal dangers of not involving their subordinates.

The ways of managing those overtly resistant to change are varied, and like the rest of our sample it was middle managers who resisted most. Many were weeded out, '*some left, early retirement, voluntary redundancy. Some didn't make the course, and the rest are now sort of business unit managers.*' In addition to retraining, more direct measures were used to get people to leave or retrain:

> *Selection by interview was part of the redundancy procedure. But you don't get a 100 per cent perfect fit for this new style, so we did a lot of profiling and found very bad fits from a psychometric point of view, very worrying. What we then decided was to go into a major training programme.* *(Employee Relations Director)*

That toeing the management line was the key to job security and career progression was never in question. The successful conversion of old-style managers was a cause of celebration, and blocks of resistance were punished.

General implications

This case study helped us make sense of the patterns of responses found in our larger sample, for with minor variations they were consistent. Managers demonstrate they are adept at familiarising themselves with and then using the fashionable terminology of the management gurus. Expressions such as: 'facilitating', 'quality-driven', 'networking', 'enabling', 'empowering', 're-engineering', 'multiskilling', 'involvement', 'participation', 'downsizing', 'communication', etc., are now commonplace in their everyday vocabulary, but are often used to describe conventional programmes of change. Such evidence can be shown to support the view that a new management model of facilitate and empower is now supplanting the outmoded methods of command and control. If correct, then today's management will be founded on consensus, voluntarism, participative experimentation and mutual adjustments.

It is possible to assert that the absence of overt resistance means that command and control management has been vanquished, and replaced by consensus and empowerment. This is because alternative interpretations that such resistance is suppressed by other factors are not readily admitted. We therefore advise caution before concluding that a major shift in management style has taken place. In the final section we again return to appraise new wave theories, in the light of the evidence we have put forward.

4.7 Conclusions

Much new wave thinking is drawn from Japanese management philosophy and practice. Without actually denying its distinctive cultural base, the influence of many important aspects is almost ignored, and little attention is drawn to the:

- continuing personal, social and commercial links between the *zaibatsu* companies that were broken up by the US occupying forces;
- very close relationships between big companies, politicians and state mandarins;
- The role of the Ministry of International Trade and Industry (MITI) in constructing and sustaining a highly successful, centrally planned economic expansion strategy, from the early 1950s.

Despite examples of the successful impact of centralised planning, it is taken for granted that a market economy, 'driven by an invisible hand', is the most efficient economic system. Hence organisations have no alternative but to 'create the dynamism of the market within' (Peters, 1992). The influence of comparable historical, cultural and institutional aspects of Western commercial rationality is hardly considered.

If problems are only seen to exist at the organisational or individual level, then it can be safely assumed that any necessary correction will be achieved by changing attitudes, practices or corporate culture – for example, by delayering and multiskilling, as described in this chapter. Responsibility for company performance can then be ascribed principally, if not exclusively, to the abilities of individual managers. The impact of politicians, banks or investors may be discounted, even though governments are routinely lobbied to pursue agendas and policies to stimulate and promote performance.

New wave management claims to transform organisational work by harnessing the creative potential of all employees, especially managers. This is achieved by instilling a strong identification with corporate objectives that include flexibility and team working, but in practice we believe the evidence suggests that bureaucracy is often strengthened, not removed or delayered.

Managers are attracted to ideas that promise improved commitment, innovation and productivity, in order to achieve competitive advantage. But there is the greatest reluctance to reform the established structure of accountability and control, with the psychological outcomes of stress, confusion, demoralisation and cynicism. While the ambition of new management thinkers is to reform the patterns of belief and behaviour in organisations, the evidence from our research suggests this ambition will not be fulfilled without making significant changes in the structures of power relations, ownership and control.

In the next chapter we concentrate on human resource management (HRM). All the research revealed that this was another area of great importance and significance to managers. In addition to examining the data we also attempt to answer questions like 'What is HRM?' and 'What is its strategic role?' The non-specialist manager might therefore find this background a useful introduction to the theory and practice of HRM.

5 Human Resource Management

5.1 Introduction

Virtually all interviewees indicated that human resource management (HRM) was a very important topic, since HRM policies and practices form a key part of the new approach to management and organisation. It is claimed that competitive advantage results from the commitment and flexibility of staff, combined with their willingness to respond rapidly to changing market conditions. This chapter therefore draws on the research data to focus on changes and continuity in HRM, while expanding on themes introduced in earlier chapters. As we introduce and define the theories and background of HRM, it is felt that the non-specialist manager will also find this section particularly useful.

However, before looking at our findings, it is important to recognise the strengths and limitations of our data. A strength lies in providing managers' reflections upon HRM that are not taken in isolation from a broader appreciation of changes in management practices. As described in Chapter 3, our open-ended interview schedule was not tightly focused upon HRM, or indeed any other specific issue. This contrasts with other studies that have tended to examine the policies and practices of HRM out of their wider management context.

We invited managers to talk generally about recent organisational change, and if they mentioned HRM-type developments, like employee involvement or empowerment, then we would ask them to elaborate. So, in the main, their accounts arose spontaneously out of a wide-ranging conversation about continuity and change, rather than in direct response to a specific and defined question about such practices.

We believe the data tell us something about how HRM policies and practices are operating within organisations. In presenting these findings we take particular themes and examine different aspects of the HRM approach to employee relations. To avoid a fragmented approach we concentrate on data from two manufacturing companies, one from the steel industry, a recently privatised utility, two financial services companies, and a vehicle assembler. When exploring the central themes of HRM we use the case study of a vehicle assembler in comparison with a financial services company.

5.2 What is human resource management?

Some would say that HRM is simply a trendy label used by personnel specialists to re-badge their existing practices, that it is little more than a new name for Personnel Management as the title of the department or manager changes, but the established practices do not. No doubt putting old wine in new bottles has occurred in many organisations, and this is especially likely as HRM becomes more widespread and fashionable.

It is important, however, to appreciate that personnel management is not static. It has developed over time, shifting from a welfare-oriented role to identify more closely with the development of techniques to secure improvements in corporate efficiency. While this might explain why HRM is a victim of the 'Alice principle', which allows a term to mean whatever an academic or practitioner wants it to mean, it does not clarify the definition by removing confusion.

However, to suggest that nothing has changed, or that HRM is a meaningless concept, overlooks the way it has reshaped the language of personnel management and how it fits with other holistic approaches to organisational change, like total quality management (TQM) and corporate culture. There are also important continuities with the historical development of personnel management, and a concern of its practitioners to boost their status and influence by being seen to contribute at a strategic level.

Personnel management has tended to be associated with problem-solving at the shop-floor level, whereas HRM is the management of all employees, including managers, and seeks to match and harmonise employment practice with market requirements. As one of our interviewees insisted, when commenting upon the change of name of his department from Personnel to Human Resource Management:

> *People thought it was just a name change but it was much more than that. It was a conscious change in the focus of the department; before it had a strong welfare role and no concept of business need or goals. My boss is now much more involved in the strategic management group whereas the previous guy wasn't at all.*
>
> *(Personnel Manager, Financial Services)*

That said, it is important to discount the often gushing tributes to HRM by consultants, academic entrepreneurs and practitioners. They all have a vested interest in exaggerating its novelty and distinctiveness, and tend to pay little attention to the translation of HRM ideas into management practices where they encounter scepticism and selectivity. There is a tendency to present HRM as if it were a coherent body of knowledge, when perhaps it more resembles 'A patchwork quilt ... stitched together from the diverse currents of change which presently impinge upon the management of the employment relationship' (Keenoy, 1990a).

These 'diverse currents' have actively contributed to contemporary changes in work organisation and, while these can be exaggerated, the intensification of competition is leading managers to explore different ways of managing. Sisson (1990) associates HRM with four features of employment practice:

- an integration of personnel policies with business planning;
- a shift in responsibility of personnel issues from specialists to senior line managers;
- a shift from the collectivism of management and trade union relations to the individualism of management to employee relations;
- an emphasis upon commitment and the exercise of initiative, with managers acting as facilitators of employee empowerment.

The movement in management thinking and practice, in which HRM plays a central role, is a shift to a more strategic approach in managing personnel, or human resources. Government policy has reduced the ability of organised labour to resist new employment practices and this enables HRM to advance a more integrated approach to their management. This is also combined with a more calculating and segmented approach to the pay and conditions of particular individuals and groups of employees.

The intent of HRM-inspired programmes is to secure increased co-operation, flexibility and productivity, by enabling employees to feel more involved, empowered and responsible for defined corporate goals. Legge (1989) helpfully identifies several common themes, suggesting that:

- Human resources policies are integrated with strategic business planning and used to reinforce an appropriate (or change an inappropriate) organisational culture.
- Human resources are valuable and a source of competitive advantage.
- Human resources may be tapped most effectively by mutually consistent policies that promote commitment and which, as a consequence, foster a willingness in employees to act flexibly in the interests of the adaptive organisation's pursuit of excellence.

When the hype of HRM is stripped away, there remains a philosophy and loosely coupled set of practices that seek, in a systematic way, to rationalise, harmonise and maximise the contribution of each employee to corporate objectives. At the heart of the process is a concern to fashion a culture and ways of working that allow employees, the human resources, to be selected, recruited and trained to achieve defined strategic goals. Guest (1991) has suggested that HRM involves:

- Raising employee commitment to corporate agendas;
- The development of greater workforce flexibility, in terms of individual employment patterns, as well as greater team working;
- Raising the quality of employees, through effective training and development programmes and strategic integration;
- Harnessing these objectives to the implementation of a corporate strategy, for which all managers are held responsible.

In drawing the notions of HRM developed by Sisson, Legge and Guest, the following interrelated elements can be seen:

- *Strategic role.* The integration of HRM policies with business planning, though a systematic approach to recruitment, training, appraisal, etc.

- *Employee involvement.* Developing a corporate culture of involvement, by shifting from institutionalised management–trade union agreements, to more flexible and co-operative management–employee relationships.
- *Employee empowerment.* Emphasising the commitment of individuals and teams who use their initiative, with managers acting as facilitators.
- *Collective managerial responsibility.* A shift in responsibility for all HRM-related issues from line specialists to all managers.

In the next four sections, we examine each of these elements in turn. While this enables us to focus in detail upon particular aspects of HRM philosophy and practice, it is important to appreciate that, in practice, all the elements are closely interrelated. For example, a strategic orientation to employee involvement is likely to be both a condition and a consequence of effective team working, individual empowerment and collective managerial responsibility.

5.2.1 *The strategic role of HRM*

Many of our interviewees cited the development of HRM policies and practices in response to major structural changes. For example, market-driven reorganisation into separate business units to reduce costs or improve responsiveness; or delayering, where an interest in team working, involvement and empowerment was considerably boosted by the problems and challenges posed by the flattening of hierarchies. In only a minority of cases did we observe the foresight of developing HR policies in advance of, or even in parallel with, changes in structure.

> *A manager's role is to motivate, energise and empower, all good modern jargon words. We are trying to change a culture of 50–100 years, to get managers to focus on people. Developing a business, technology or a financial strategy is easy. It's the most difficult thing in the world to create a people strategy and actually put it into effect.*
>
> *(Group MD, Privatised Utility)*

Such reflections suggest why business strategy is often developed in advance of an HRM strategy or is at best only loosely coupled to it, a similar story being told by other interviewees who were not talking hypothetically but about developments in their own companies. Attention to the culture very often tended to follow major structural change, rather than being integrated with it.

Many similar accounts of HRM suggest it is often not strategic, in the sense of being planned and integrated into business policy. Rather, it is often an expedient or unco-ordinated response to unexpected problems resulting from strategic decisions to restructure. In some cases HRM policies and practices are of marginal importance to strategic planning – for example, using specialists to improve recruitment quality, or improving the competencies of existing staff and linking corporate performance with career advancement.

Companies often flirt with HRM techniques, like team work and networking, but use them in a limited and unsystematic way to train employees and transfer business values. Only infrequently did this form part of a wider programme of organisational change, the emphasis being on up-skilling and limited delayering, rather than the integration of HRM into business strategy. One executive put it more directly as follows:

> *We are looking to improve the quality of staff and at the end of the day it is like improving the output of a machine. If it is more efficient and produces more then you don't require as many machines and that ultimately has to be the objective.*
>
> *(Senior Executive, Staff Development, Manufacturing)*

In a minority of companies there was a conscious effort to pre-design HRM into the corporate strategy and others where, although this was the intention, it was prevented. One obstacle was a dim recognition by senior managers that assessing human resource capabilities is relevant when determining strategy, or that achieving particular strategic goals is often conditional upon developing employees with appropriate core competencies.

This recognition was comparatively well advanced at a financial services company, where its senior managers had met to determine the core values that should guide their activity and approach to business. The outcome was the identification of three basic areas: employees, clients and business performance:

> *With people, a value is placed upon having clear roles and accountabilities. An equal opportunities environment, where employees are committed, enthusiastic and involved, taking responsibility for their contribution to growth and future success. Clients attach a value to our honesty, integrity and service standards, which leads to trust and long-*

term relationships For business performance, we must be able to deliver on our commitments, achieving the range of performance measures negotiated with our parent, and growing the underlying value of our company. (*Director of Human Resources, Financial Services*)

Each of these three areas is associated with a number of key competencies that must be acquired and displayed for the values to be realised (Table 5.1).

Table 5.1 Key competencies

Area	Key competencies
People	Team morale; developing staff; influencing; open communication; empowerment
Clients	Meeting customer needs; quality standards; change management; application of expertise; building relationships
Business performance	Commitment; planning; monitoring and controlling; decision-making; innovation; breadth of perspective

Managers at the company subsequently reported that changes in organisation and business methods had been directly guided by the senior managers' interpretations of the meaning of these values. However, it is also relevant to note the personnel manager's assessment that these changes were prompted by the recession and *'would never have occurred if we had been in an expansionist mode'*.

The recession suspended translation of these core values into organisational change, while performance failure meant the Managing Director was 'let go', and we were told he was resistant to an earlier attempt to introduce HRM. A sense of crisis was seen from the exceptional redundancy of many employees, including middle managers. This gave senior management the opportunity to drive the core values through the organisation, with minimal staff opposition. In this case, business strategy has been shaped and directed by core values that are also being used to restructure the organisation and develop HRM policies.

Such integration was the exception, however, not the rule, as companies usually responded after the event. Nevertheless, as we suggest later in this chapter, trying to integrate business strategy with HRM is not necessarily either ethically or commercially effective, for while it may be very appealing in theory, it proves to be difficult to put into practice.

5.2.2 *Employee involvement*

In many firms, an interest in involvement and team working arose from problems caused by delayering. For example, in financial services, where strategy and HRM were most integrated, we were told that between 20 and 30 levels still remained, even after redundancies. This was seen as unsatisfactory, implying that more levels meant less individual discretion and responsibility, a problem that was being examined but had yet to be resolved.

Delayering also limits promotion opportunities. Without defined career paths it is harder to retain and motivate ambitious, well-qualified staff. Inappropriate reward systems just exacerbate the problem. The vehicle assembler changed the payment structure, so that each grade had a wider band to allow for salary increases, but without promotion to a higher grade. But this demotivated those who measured their contribution, progress and sense of satisfaction in terms of promotion. We return to issues of pay and motivation in Chapter 7.

HRM specialists are often asked for 'solutions'. How can staff be encouraged to evaluate themselves differently? A new focus on job satisfaction also coincided with a change to business units and cross-functional teams, where it was assumed that breaking up the old functional structure *'will develop broader and better managers and have an indirect benefit on their development in job satisfaction'*. Managers seem to hope that the new system will somehow be self-correcting. Staff will be given more responsibility and opportunities to extend skills like *'personality, communication, influence and persuasion'* by lateral movement. It is hoped this development, together with participation in cross-departmental teams, will then substitute greater job satisfaction for promotion.

In many companies that we visited the human resource problems associated with delayering and reorganisation are recognised, along with the difficulties of identifying effective solutions. The assumption, or hope, is that the demands on employees will be viewed positively, as challenges rather than imposed pressures, and so make greater job satisfaction replace promotion. Changing the structure, and exhorting staff to greater efforts, was insufficient, so more responsibility and accountability are ways in which to involve employees. Individually and collectively they are encouraged to 'own their work', and to be creative and innovative, using their initiative.

Many managers saw team working as a means of getting employees involved in identifying and solving organisational problems of poor communication, inadequate co-ordination and limited responsiveness. Many firms recruited or used consultants to run team work courses. Even if team working was not identified as a way of evaluating and developing managers, it was seen as important for achieving business objectives.

Increasing employee involvement does not simply mean encouraging them to become more committed or caring about work quality. Employee involvement can also be a means of sharing the responsibility for problems managers have been unable to solve. Using or involving employees as unpaid, but extremely well-informed, 'consultants' is clearly attractive to senior managers. It was suggested that this is why the Japanese have a competitive advantage:

> *You have got to create the 'participative-type' company; we believe that's what the Japanese are doing. I'm on about participation in the fabric of the organisation. Essentially the key is that people come up with solutions, not receive them.*
>
> *(Employee Relations Director, Vehicle Assembly)*

Another senior manager at this plant connected an emphasis on employee involvement with the eventual demise of management as controllers of labour. He predicted that as employees accept more responsibility and become more self-disciplined, so they will control themselves. We found the idea of self-discipline as a recurrent and key theme of employee involvement programmes.

5.2.3 *Employee empowerment*

Empowerment, also seen as a consequence of delayering, was mentioned by virtually all interviewees. Getting employees to take more responsibility and be accountable was seen as a key way to improve productivity and quality: *'The term we use is empowering the*

workforce.... Empowerment, I suppose, really is the key word.'
(Employee Relations Director, Vehicle Assembly)

Empowerment is key because, as managers become facilitators, it is a means of connecting corporate strategy with HRM practices and policies. It captures the assumption that individuals and groups are encouraged or required to become more involved in decision-making. From a managerial perspective, employees are empowered when they behave in ways that are more responsive to corporate values and objectives without supervision or direction.

Empowerment may be achieved by developing systems and cultures that release the creativity and flexibility of employees, but in a controlled and predetermined way. The use of information and communication technologies to regulate work scheduling, and reduce the need for close supervision, was also called empowerment. It was suggested that these systems would enable employees to organise and accomplish complex tasks themselves. Instead of being a clerical worker processing information, but referring complex problems to others, the employee becomes a service consultant, or a proficient user of sophisticated IT packages that take care of most of these problems.

Using IT, it is possible to replace costly specialists, like underwriters, with expert systems, software that aids decision-making. This concentrates diverse activities into the role of a 'service consultant'. This is, however, represented as the empowerment of clerical workers, rather than the redundancy of specialists based on the power of new technology. It is apparent that the activity of the service consultant is no less structured, and allows very little increased discretion over the clerical worker. In fact, new technology allows managers to structure tasks more precisely and to monitor productivity more accurately, so that such service consultants may actually be seen as 'clerks', despite the title: *'The supervisor allocates the work knowing how many clerks have turned up. The system leads them step by step and provides the data and decision skills, they don't have to ask anyone.'*
(Assistant General Manager (IT), Financial Services)

This example suggests that caution should be exercised when reviewing claims that employees are being empowered by changes in organisational structures and working practices. In many cases, it seemed that empowerment was being used to mean increased responsibility and accountability. Competition was a driver to reduce costs, improve quality and be adaptable, and a way to achieve these goals is to require employees to be more productive by taking on tasks previously done by others. This process of absorption, rationalisation and intensification is much more attractively described as empowerment.

One director in the vehicle assembly company gave us his understanding of how the organisation had to be changed to enable empowerment to develop and become harnessed to business objectives. He used some jargon from Peters and Waterman (1982), who summarise their concept of excellence in terms of 'loose-tight' properties – that is, a structure loose enough to allow some discretion and responsibility, yet sufficiently tight to ensure that empowerment is directed to the achievement of corporate goals. To achieve this 'loose-tight' structure the company had been reorganised into business units, *'a series of businesses within a business, where each of the former production managers is sort of a mini-MD, where there's autonomous working'*.

But how far this ideal of 'loose-tight' properties had actually become 'autonomous working' was in doubt. While acknowledging that considerable progress had been made in empowering the shop floor, who were gradually becoming much more involved and self-disciplined, we found an aversion by senior management to devolving responsibility to the business unit managers:

> *We should tell the business unit managers, 'That's your budget, improve it by 5 per cent year-on-year, how you please.' The weakest part of empowerment at the moment is the reluctance to let go of some of these things at the very senior level.*
>
> *(Employee Relations Director, Vehicle Assembly)*

This criticism of the limited empowerment of business unit managers was not confined to expressions of concern about a missed opportunity to reduce costs. It was also identified as a source of demotivation and confusion, since it seemed to contradict company policy. Not 'letting go' was sending a different message, despite business unit managers being seen as key to the new organisational structure. Without their full confidence, the drive to achieve continuous improvement through empowerment was being put in jeopardy.

This brings us to a consideration of the fourth element of HRM policies and practices, the diffusion of responsibility from specialists to all managers.

5.2.4 *Collective managerial responsibility*

Under HRM, employees are seen as resources that can be developed, being capable, with guidance and training, of taking on additional responsibilities. There is still a concern to keep employee costs down and to weaken any challenge to the managerial prerogative, but at the same time there is a shift from close supervision to individual or team responsibility for meeting targets. The successful implementation of HRM-type policies and practices, therefore, depends upon new managerial styles. Managers must be willing and able to identify and facilitate the acquisition of the appropriate attitudes, competencies and skills required to produce this self-disciplined workforce.

The importance of getting all managers committed to this new philosophy is shown by the following example, which describes an intense campaign of management development, by communication and training, initiated in 1991:

> *A brief sabbatical at a business school convinced me that command and control was really dead and that we needed to get managers to change their behaviour in four areas. Communication, Empowerment. Recognition of potential and Positivity, which means 'Yes, we can do that', not 'I would like you to do this' or 'seeing all the problems.*
>
> *(Group MD, Privatised Utility)*

Since the managers would be directly responsible for putting this theory into practice, a notable feature of this campaign was that they ran it themselves. This was to deal with the complaint that *'it's not like that when you get back to work'*, being in contrast to a series of earlier programmes which were run externally by professional trainers.

Delayering was not simply viewed as reducing staff costs, but as a way to get managers to do things rather than to check what others are doing. We found a similar picture at most other companies we visited: *'We're not so much aiming to take out hierarchy as to take out bureaucracy.' (Managing Director, Vehicle Assembly)*

This objective was met by creating business unit managers and a programme of cross-functional training for ex-supervisors, but the cost reduction motive was also still present. It was acknowledged that once team operation in the business units had evolved, and the specialist skills transferred between their members, then it would be time to re-examine the structure.

When the new system beds down it is assumed that *'slack will be generated, opportunities for designing out the need for these people'*. As we keep stressing, underneath the rhetoric the evidence suggests that we frequently find other agendas.

5.3 *Tensions in HRM*

At one level HRM means that issues like recruitment, induction, reward, training and promotion, are all integrated to achieve maximum co-operation. Central to this objective is the development of working practices and forms of motivation that increase employee flexibility and work quality. But, at another level, packages of rewards, training, appraisal and promotion are segmented to fit the markets for the particular grades of labour required for any given task. So where labour is plentiful and the tasks simple, the package is reduced or, if the converse, it is increased, to match supply and demand.

The promotion of an organisation-wide approach of mutuality and commitment from all staff sits uneasily with a selective approach offering different packages. There is a tension between the idea that all employees should be treated as valued human resources and commercial or market pressures. The emblem 'Human Resource Management' suggests that the contribution of human beings is of key importance, as summed up in the catch phrase, 'people are our most important asset'. But the fact that HRM is part of corporate strategy also implies that employment practice will be driven by business objectives.

Consequently, within the HRM approach and philosophy, there are inconsistencies and tensions. Human resources will be valued and policies adopted only in so far as they are calculated to be compatible with achieving those objectives – which, in turn, means that there are likely to be recurrent tensions between developing an organisation in which *'people are committed, enthusiastic and involved in their work'* and organising work in ways that ensure that the company is achieving its *'range of performance measures'*. *(Company Newspaper, Financial Services)*

The history of management is littered with such attempts to reconcile the priorities of employees with the requirements of employers and owners. These range from Taylorism, or Scientific Management, which promised to raise employee earnings through training and performance-related pay, through to 'Corporate Culture', which promised to raise employee commitment and morale. This research suggests that HRM may be just another such attempt since, while it is a departure from such practices, it is clearly not a quantum leap.

Significant differences were found between companies. Some manufacturers are training operators and managers to cover the gap created by removing supervisors and other hierarchical levels. At the other extreme is an approach which requires all employees to show commitment to the core values or leave, a tough line that may be justified by the external context, such as competition:

> *Organisations in our sector are taking out levels, so I think we also need to be competitive. It's also our new culture, a set of core values defining very clearly how we shall operate and behave. People will accept these values, if they don't they should move on.*
> *(Personnel Manager, Financial Services)*

Most companies are enthusiastic to establish common values, but this drive seems to be tempered by many factors, including a pragmatic approach which views some aspects of HRM, like its anti-union thrust, with some scepticism:

> *Some senior managers want unions as it's easier to negotiate with one group. I've probably drifted to where I'd be happy without them, but wouldn't want them not to exist, because I believe the biggest risk is an over-powerful management can lead to abuse of the individual. A difficult balance, as on the other hand they can be a bloody nuisance and waste a lot of time.* *(Managing Director, Steel)*

We have already pointed out that conflicts in HRM must be managed if the effort to integrate and motivate employees is not to be undermined, e.g. how to reward individuals for exceptional performance versus collective team working, or when work flexibility conflicts with an individual's sense of identity as a specialist or craftsman. Much of the practical activity involved in devising and implementing an HRM approach is directed at handling such tensions.

However, the HRM philosophy encourages a belief that such tensions will be resolved when its policies are working, so that any difficulties are then attributed to an incomplete or imperfect implementation. Alternatively, problems may be seen as personal weaknesses, or a consequence of external impersonal forces. If individuals fail to respond appropriately their removal can be rationalised in terms of collective responsibility and tough love:

> *Consider those who've given 25–30 years and are not going any further, not the wankers you fire, but those whose competencies don't meet the new challenges. We must make room for those who can. So I devised a package they find difficult to refuse, two-thirds pension plus five years. You put that to a guy who's working his balls off with a lot of problems, knows he's slowing down and has got real good people coming behind, he can think, 'Well, fine, I can go at the top. I've done a good job. I can go out with a warm glow and some financial security.'*
>
> *(Group Managing Director, Privatised Utility)*

'Letting them go' improves the job security of other staff and it presents the redundant with a fresh opportunity to find employment in a situation where their particular contribution would be more greatly valued. So it may be that employees will respond uncritically, if not very enthusiastically, to the populist appeal of HRM, and accept its seemingly altruistic logic of tough love. It is also not difficult to find redundant executives who celebrate the day they were let go, because this freed them to do other things they now find more rewarding.

However, will other employees unreservedly endorse new relationships and be loyal and committed, knowing they will be quickly dismissed if their contribution no longer fits corporate needs? This is a paradox, for apparent trust is required, as for example in TQM programmes. It seems more likely that the lack of opposition comes from high unemployment, weakened trade unions and the absence of labour legislation, rather than a widespread support for HRM. After his eulogy on 'the warm glow', the Group MD spontaneously added:

> *Now, you can't do that with main layers who are on £200 a week, you*

just can't, but main layers aren't the problem. We have got to get movement at the top of the business. We'll be doing more of that.

At the heart of the problem of transforming the ideals of HRM into practical realities is the employment contract between employers and employees, whose interests coincide and conflict. Employees want an income, while owners and managers want to hire and train employees, including managers. Each is dependent on the other for securing their respective objectives. The inevitable conflict is between employers trying to maximise staff effort for minimum reward and employees being interested in the reverse. Moreover, the reward–effort bargaining is indeterminate. The employer's challenge is to devise a system that ensures that sufficient productive effort is made for the reward paid and that this system is perceived to be fair and legitimate by employees.

5.4 *The significance of the employment contract*

The following example shows the stress and tension of employment in a company where staff were expected to live its core values, whether at work or in their leisure time. As part of a character- and team-building activity, teams of employees were asked to participate, Japanese-style, in a variety of extramural activities. For some managers, such exercises were an unqualified virtue and benefit, as in the following example:

The week in the Scottish Highlands was a brilliant exercise. I saw a group of individuals go away, all in their own little pigeon-holes, an accountant, an actuary, an IT guy. What came back was really a team of people that knew each other and had much higher trust levels. That was a terrific input for that group.

This assessment was not shared by his colleague, who declined an invitation to a later 'weekend break' because *'I couldn't think of a more boring thing to do.'* But he also interpreted the invitation as an instruction that he would have difficulty in refusing. He couldn't help feeling that *'my absence will be strongly noticed'*, but he still refused and not just because of boredom. More importantly, he saw it as an imposition on his free time and symptomatic of a company that required allegiance to its core values at all times. Its employees were expected to completely internalise these and then act accordingly. *'That's where I'm uncomfortable, I must admit. That's where*

I think I would draw the line. The values are going so far that you need to display these socially.'

For him, there was an important distinction between what he was prepared to do in working hours and his free time, when he could do and be what he chose. He began the interview by describing himself as a *'human resource professional'*, who was *'completely transferable between sectors'*. Later he made a clear distinction between those 'professionals' like himself, and other managers who played along with whatever was expected of them, but were highly regarded because they displayed the right behaviours. The cosmopolitan professionals were reluctant to ally themselves closely with the company values, except where they coincided with their own professional commitments.

> *We have many problems with managers who are the least effective, but have actually taken on board the values with the most vigour. They behave as required by the new culture. It's a cynical exercise. These guys have been here for fifteen years and they have hardly done a day's work in their life, but they have played the political game.*
> *(Human Resource Manager, Financial Services)*

Assuming this interpretation is correct, and not just an expression of frustration and resentment, then it suggests that a capacity and willingness to 'play the political game' can count for more than working effectively. Instead of correcting ineffectiveness, the apparent strengthening of corporate culture conceals and promotes it. Those whose careers or competencies leave them with little option but to stay with the company are obliged to behave appropriately. Others, with more options and, paradoxically perhaps, more to contribute, do not accept the degree of corporate cultural control being imposed on them. Being more likely to challenge this, they risk being silenced or ostracised, but certainly are more likely to move to another company. The effect is thus counterproductive.

5.5 Conclusions

The evidence has demonstrated why HRM is a result of tensions in the employment relationship, as well as being yet another attempt to manage them. Its policies are promoted as a modern, progressive way of weakening resistance to the managerial prerogative, and they promise to reconstruct the employment contract by involving and empowering employees. HRM techniques will enable staff, or human resources, to be fully reconciled to organisational goals and then to work effectively to achieve them. This means they can then be flexibly deployed, with minimum resistance to any changes, to gain and sustain maximum competitive advantage, so securing profitable growth.

Our data suggests that HRM can be effective in securing competitive advantage when it succeeds in reducing, suppressing and glossing tensions in the employment relationship, at least when labour legislation is weak and government economic policy deflationary. For precisely these reasons it is nevertheless a mistake to identify the potency of enlightened HRM policies and practices as a primary cause of any new understanding between employers and employees.

It is necessary to put the successes of HRM in a wider context, as shown by the survey data and the views echoed by many interviewees. They identified the political climate and economic recession as crucial for generating the conditions that made HRM viable, as this final quote testifies:

> *We've used the crisis, in the economy, the recession, world markets and so on. Nothing wrong with the crisis. That's helped us to do many things. We've used that to get people on our side, particularly the trade unions and our employees. And we've just kept pushing.*
> *(Employee Relations Director, Vehicle Assembly)*

It seems reasonably likely that the underlying tensions have been temporarily subdued rather than permanently eliminated. They continue to be manifest in diverse forms of organisational politics and, while this is true, most implementations of HRM will be selective and moderated by the practical politics of organisational change and employee resistance. HRM is also likely to be used as a political football, because managers routinely deploy their influence and discretion to interpret, support and implement those policies and practices they see best fitting their own values and priorities, or which they calculate can be productively used in pursuit of their own ambitions.

Despite some interdependence, the reality of the employment contract is that even empowered employees neither own nor control the organisation of work. Therefore, when push comes to shove, they are hired, deployed and fired as disposable commodities. Knowledge of this disposability means commitment to the organisation is likely to be conditional and that co-operation results as much from material dependence as any other form of consent. Our evidence supports Guest's view (1987), that a full and unequivocal commitment to the consensual ideals of HRM is likely to await 'a much more radical shift in ownership and control in industry'.

Given that such a shift has not yet occurred, and is not even in prospect, managers are asked to make sense of these tensions and work round them. As we have already suggested, however, their biggest problem is that the necessary awareness and analysis of these tensions is marginalised, if not actually suppressed, by the HRM theorists and its more zealous evangelists. If HRM is incapable of acknowledging conflicts that are part and parcel of the employment contract, then it is ill equipped to address the practical issue of organisational politics.

In the next chapter we briefly look at management change in financial services. We focus on some of the differences to be found when dramatic change is imposed on organisations that are used to operating in a rigid, highly bureaucratic way and within well-understood traditional and institutionalised settings.

6 Management Changes in Financial Services

6.1 Introduction

This chapter takes a brief look at the UK financial services sector to expand upon some of the differences identified earlier. These mature organisations exemplify the attempt rapidly to transform organisations with long-established and highly bureaucratic hierarchies with rigid administrative controls. This industry used to be characterised by a very comfortable and predictable environment, but this was dramatically overturned in the mid-1980s, following economic deregulation and political re-regulation through the Financial Services Act.

This legislation effectively created a new more integrated sector, as the traditional differences between banks, building societies and insurance companies was removed. So 'bancassurance' developed as banks, or building societies, offered their own insurance products as well as banking services. In addition, formalised cartels were replaced by intense competition. Almost overnight, managers and staff were expected to respond flexibly to these new market conditions, where customer service and quality now mattered for competitive differentiation. Consumers became increasingly financially sophisticated, aware and demanding. In part this resulted from the extra publicity generated by the often negative consequences of change within the industry.

Thus it is instructive to look at this sector and see how such dramatic change is being managed against the historical and cultural context. While many of the approaches to change discussed in this chapter were apparent in manufacturing and retailing, there certainly seem to be significant differences.

In financial services managers have been removed or delayered, but not to the same extent or in quite the same way as in other sectors. In manufacturing the shop floor had tended to be empowered, but at the expense of delayered middle and junior managers. In the financial services firms we researched there was more evidence of the empowerment of managerial staff, but ironically those managers that remained were being empowered to manage their subordinates more intensively.

6.2 Competition and change

While initially directed at the manufacturing sector, the same ideas of new wave management have been taken up in the financial services sector. With a dramatic intensification of competition, the same prescriptions of improved flexibility, strong organisational culture and enhanced quality have been seized upon. One important difference from manufacturing is the nature of 'production', for the outputs of financial services organisations are effectively intangible. They are a set of largely perishable performances which are perceived by the consumer, rather than handled or used as defined objects.

Moreover, many of these outputs are produced and consumed simultaneously, while their delivery is often highly labour-intensive, through multiple retail outlets. Such heterogeneity implies that performance standards may vary between individuals and branches, and from day to day. The overall 'package' is often subsumed into ideas of service and quality, with some measurable aspects and a large subjective content of emotive meaning.

With apparently very similar lending and saving products, few discernible sources of differentiation are available, though deregulation provided the impetus for financial services companies to competitively differentiate. Research by Smith and Harbisher (1989) found that, while banks are generally perceived as distinct from building societies, within these categories the organisations remained relatively undifferentiated. There was thus pressure for organisations to change and respond to competition, but many were uncertain as to how to proceed.

In general, banks were seen as more professional, while building societies were friendlier, suggesting that a way forward could be to build on the distinctive customer-friendly notion while creating a professional financial services image.

Perceptions of identity and image have thus emerged as new corporate concerns, perhaps to a greater extent than is typical in the manufacturing sector. Moreover, these became conflated with related issues, such as organisational culture, customer care, service and quality.

We have already established that a voluminous prescriptive literature urges managers to change what they do. If there are only a few studies relating to manufacturing that seek to question and evaluate that literature, then it will be appreciated that studies are even more sparse in financial services. Hence, although necessarily limited and only a small part of the whole project, we nevertheless feel that useful and valuable insights are gained by examining changes in management practices in organisations that are outside the more common manufacturing research site.

To establish the background context we first consider two quotes, noting that, as all interviewees are in financial services, only their job title is given:

> *We've had workshops looking at quality and productivity, actually targeting people now. We're going to a Ford-type environment now, and we wouldn't have related this a few years ago to banking.*
> *(Service Manager)*

> *With increased uncertainty, the intensification of national competition is the key issue facing top management in financial services, along with growing demands from customers.* *(General Manager)*

Within companies, much organisational orthodoxy has been subject to intense scrutiny in an attempt to achieve increased competitiveness in terms of both the quality and costs of service. Activities not seen to add value, including some bureaucratic controls, have been undermined, if not entirely abandoned. Those remaining activities are reassessed in a continual programme of process redesign.

> *In my early days it was very rigidly structured and quite inflexible. We were absolutely bound by books of rules which it was virtually a cardinal sin not to adhere to. I mean, we have procedures now, and they are fairly strict, but there is some allowance made for innovation.*
> *(Department Head)*

Organisational fat has been cut out so that much more may be extracted from each employee. A number of different specific changes have been introduced in different organisations to bring about improved performance, and a number of different rationales have been employed to justify them. We now examine these changes and their justifications in more detail.

6.3 Change and its justification

For some companies, particular systems have been deployed to enhance efficiency and effectiveness in specific areas of their business. It seems that very little lip service is paid to the new wave management jargon, and managers are happy to justify the changes they have made in terms of profitability alone. This approach to change is most pronounced in small companies and in both the financial services and the manufacturing and retail sectors. In such organisations, changes tend to be instrumental and pragmatically aligned to the business.

Commitment to organisational goals is frequently achieved through a re-engineering of the remuneration package. Concepts like 'flexibility' are occasionally invoked when describing changes, but the majority of initiatives are simply justified by the need for profitable operation of the business: *'The first thing we did was remove all overtime and put in flexible working hours. In other words, flexible in terms of how the company requires them. First of all we put people on a shift system.' (Director)*

Rather more interesting changes are under way in larger organisations. Here, although managers see the changes as necessary for profitable trading and survival, they are also justified in terms of the humanistic ideals associated with job enrichment programmes. More 'guru-style' managerial language is invoked, as changes are perceived to be *'driven by external influences as we go through a major revolution, and a lot of those sacred cows would've had to have been thrown out of the window anyway. Suddenly there is a challenge out there.' (Managing Director)*

But changes are also justified in other terms like culture and core values, even though competition is often identified as the driver of the changes. The descriptions of change often include the suggestion or idea that there is some 'better' way to manage. The managers certainly see benefits in strictly economic terms, but are keen to play up the humanism and professional responsibility that they argue underlie the changes. We now focus on these aspects of change for the remainder of this chapter.

6.4 Change and the traditional hierarchy

One of the first issues to be tackled was the rigid and inflexible administrative control that characterised the financial services industry.

To move away from such historically deeply rooted practices was seen to be necessary in an increasingly competitive climate, but it required an extra effort because of the inbuilt resistance to any change. In most cases that we examined this push came from a new top-management team.

For example, in the personal investment subsidiary of a large high-street bank, changes were perceived to be the result of an influx of senior managers, brought in to sort out the *'restrictive old regime ... which had a detrimental effect on the business'*. When the subsidiary was set up it *'was masterminded by one man, brought in from outside along with a whole new team of people. You could say the old guard was given its marching orders.' (Department Head)*

For most of the large financial services organisations we examined, this shift occurred before the onset of recession, during the boom years of the mid-to-late 1980s. For some the move away from *'a paternalistic, dictatorial regime'* was simply the result of *'different managers with different attitudes'* moving up the organisational hierarchy: *'My management training was about staff communication, encouragement rather than fear, and I suppose as that generation move up the management chain some of that must have stuck.' (General Manager)*

For others, the explanation was to be found in terms of the large expansion of work caused by the boom. There was simply too much work and not enough time to manage in the same old way. These circumstances were pronounced for the personal investments subsidiary mentioned above. As a new branch of the parent organisation it was struggling to establish itself in an expanding market. The 'restrictive' regime inhibited flexibility, and flexibility and multiskilling were seen to be essential for success while rapidly expanding: *'There's greater flexibility that came of necessity. In a new organisation that was expanding quite rapidly, people had to become multiskilled at all sorts of things and turn your hand to whatever came up.' (Department Head)*

Concepts of flexibility and innovation were invoked in a number of organisations to enable a break with the rule book and allow business growth to take advantage of the boom. Over-extension was a result as the boom ended, with a very uncertain future in prospect. Controls and procedures were once again seen to be important, and quality also came to the fore:

> *As things settled down we did flow charts and wrote procedural manuals, then we put in a more structured system of management controls. So with that stable base we had the opportunity to start looking at quality and trying to continually improve that.*
> *(Department Manager)*

Increasing competitive pressures ensured that quality programmes were explicitly linked to improvements in productivity and cost reductions. We now examine how these moves were integrated into changes in accountability which, as before, was tied into notions of empowerment.

6.5 Empowerment and accountability

Our survey and interview evidence suggests that the relaxation of tight administrative controls in financial services organisations during the boom years of the mid-80s was not entirely reversed in the subsequent recession. Instead, new administrative procedures were implemented, and then supplemented with improved accountability, in an effort to restore managerial control. Two distinct organisational approaches to this project are apparent in our sample. In some organisations, relatively unrestrained managers and staff were reorganised and marshalled through common aims and ideals that were deployed through increased communication and training:

> *Great efforts now make sure everyone knows our business strategy, how we're going to do things. It's attitude as well; I mean, it becomes a way of life to try to tell people what to do and how to do it.*
> *(Department Head)*

On a general level employees were told what to do, and then

allowed to apply their appropriate knowledge and skills to the specifics of the business. The common ideology and language that these processes have encouraged were seen to have enabled empowerment of both staff and managers. Those individuals who were uncomfortable with the new ways of working were removed by early redundancy programmes and organisational restructuring: *'People who've been here for quite a few years haven't found it easy to adapt to changes. So they're slowly being retired or moved to the areas they should be in.' (Assistant General Manager)*

Those that remained could now take decisions, because they were deemed to be taking them in the right way, according to the right criteria. Thus, although the nature of control is altered, it has not been removed. Rather, control is displaced into personal development activities and the design of systems and self-discipline that would eventually make directive, bureaucratic control unnecessary.

Given the high costs of the established and over-managed procedures, the changes found a dual justification in both humanistic ideals and improved cost performance.

Many aspects of this approach to change were also found in companies from other sectors, although the extent of the established bureaucracy prior to the changes seems less evident. In the manufacturing organisations we investigated, we commonly found a fundamental belief in technical systems of control. In the financial services companies we perceived that, to allow flexibility and empowerment of employees at the bottom of the hierarchy, this philosophy is now being gradually applied in an environment that, traditionally, has been comparatively cosy and immune from intense competitive pressure. Such changes were seen to be particularly pronounced for managers:

> *Within the last few years a very radical culture has emerged, where we look at what we do now and then we constantly review it. The old way was stable, you knew what you were doing because somebody had been doing that for the last 10 or 20 years. Not a lot of management technique was required, it was a case of everything ticking over. Now it's the competition, you know, you've got to look at the competition.*
>
> *(Service Manager)*

For some of our interviewees, this bureaucratic hangover was seen to reflect the peculiarities of money-based products. While clerks continue to be replaced by computer systems, the bureaucratic control that dominated office environments is harder to remove: *'Our products are money products. In this company it's money in and money out.' (Assistant General Manager)*

For some of the companies, change agendas based on the new wave managerial rhetoric were deployed to strengthen bureaucratic control. It seems probable that individuals at many levels in financial service organisations are working to preserve elements of a familiar and comfortable ethos and style. These issues are exemplified by the remarks made by interviewees from life assurance, considered in more detail below, where changes seem to have taken place in an interesting way, with empowerment being restricted to the middle levels of the hierarchy.

6.6 *Managerial empowerment and accountability*

One life assurance company was trying to re-engineer a bureaucratic 'civil service' type of mentality into a profit-seeking ethos.

It was about to embark upon a quality initiative that had been preceded by a move towards results-driven management. Staff were expected to produce results and were then measured against them. This move was seen to be particularly important for those in the middle of the hierarchy, who allegedly had tended to assume that they could just sit there and pontificate. The introduction of such measures was seen to be the route by which such managers would rediscover their managerial responsibilities. They would be encouraged:

> *to control the work of the people they're managing. We've installed what is fundamentally a very simple work measurement system. It actually starts to empower and demand of the managers at all levels that they actually present in a consistent and quantifiable form what's going on in their area and then account for themselves against that plan.*
> *(Managing Director)*

> *It's about planning and control and responsibility and accountability. It's giving the front-line managers the tools to actually manage because they haven't had the tools in the past to act that way.*
> *(General Manager)*

Accountability and empowerment were terms applied to changes to managers' work, not the work of their staff. Managers were empowered and accountable for an increased managerial role over their subordinates. This was necessary because *'the workload has increased dramatically'*. Improved control was seen to be required for better performance, but the changes were still described in terms of new wave language, although for some this sometimes went too far.

The Managing Director quoted above saw empowerment as necessary for first-line managers, while for the assistant general manager the term smacked too much of a loss of control, particularly if it was to refer to those at the bottom of the hierarchy: *'Oh, we're talking about the dreaded empowerment are we? We've started to mutter about it and I fear that will all come, hopefully slowly.'*

With the absence of the training and communication used in other companies, empowerment of individuals at the very bottom of the organisational hierarchy was not an option. In other organisations, empowerment was seen as a route to the increased productivity of subordinates, but there was little confidence that they would do the *'right things'*.

6.7 Conclusions

Many of the initiatives and changes discussed in this chapter were also present in the rest of our sample. The biggest differences between the sectors would seem to be in the hierarchical level being empowered by the changes and in the form it is seen to take. Manufacturing organisations have tended to focus on the empowerment of the shop floor at the expense of junior and middle management, which is extensively delayered. Managers have also been removed in the financial services organisations we looked at, but not in anything like the same numbers. While this may be simply a quirk of our sample it could also be a reflection of a genuine difference.

This may be evidence of a fundamentally different approach, or may simply reflect a failure by top management in financial services in their attempts to re-engineer staff behaviour. Replacing direct managerial intervention is too big a jump for many financial services companies, who continue to see their staff as needing bureaucratic management. Blockers to these changes have been removed from the middle of the hierarchy in some financial services organisations, but our survey and interviews suggest that there are many still wedded to aspects of the old style at the very top. Middle managers in manufacturing organisations may have initially proved more pliable, but in the long run, it will perhaps be middle managers in financial services who will serve as facilitators in the creation of self-managing teams. That is becoming the new role model in many manufacturing companies, but more research is required to verify this point.

In the next and final chapter, we review the implications for management accounting of the changes discussed in this report.

7 Implications for Management Accounting

7.1 Introduction

As an illustrative, rather than exhaustive, concluding chapter we draw together the research findings to reflect on the implications and challenges of organisational change for the management accounting function and its practices. We first hint, in broad terms, at the extent to which the role of management accounting in organisations is perceived to be changing. Then, somewhat arbitrarily to facilitate both presentation and analysis, we take three emergent themes as subsections. The first is how empowerment and increased accountability relate to accounting and its role in achieving change. A similar approach then considers the issues raised by motivation and remuneration, and how accounting should respond.

Finally, we consider wider implications of the new organisation for the design and use of management accounting systems, particularly the contradictions that exist between those incremental changes that appear to be under way in the accounting function and the more fundamental transformations that the new organisation implies. While there seems to be little or no evidence of a basic change of emphasis in the accounting function, yet, if the gurus and their managerial supporters are to be believed, it is just such a change that the new organisation requires.

7.2 Changes in management accounting

Before addressing the three main themes, we first take a broad look at the evidence to determine the extent to which the role of management accounting in organisations is perceived to be changing. Although our interviewees were not asked explicit questions about accounting, either in general or in their own organisations, these issues sometimes emerged, almost as an inevitable fact of life. Comments were made about how accounting practices used to be taken at face value but that now these were being questioned. *'The old ways of doing accounting'* were perceived as being of little relevance to the new organisational realities:

> *The accountant can sit upstairs and crunch the numbers and simply provide a set of management accounts and your statutory accounts. He'll have them audited, all neat and tidy, but it's reporting history and has very little meaning in managing the business.*
>
> *(Managing Director, Automotive)*

Some comments picked up and reflected the idea of flexibility, with many complaining or lamenting that the rigidity of accounting practices did not fit with the new, more fluid organisation. In essence, our interviewees complained of the arbitrariness of allocating costs, observing how management accounting tries to *'put everything in predetermined or fixed boxes'* which did little *'to help determine cause or effect'*. The standard approach to costing was challenged, especially the idea that any cost could be 'fixed'. Equally, however, it was appreciated that marginal costing, concentrating on contribution analysis and variable costs, had limitations and could *'create a lot of problems'*: *'The principles are fine but running the business on the basis of some fairly arbitrary allocation of costs, even though there might be some logic behind them, is very inappropriate.' (Managing Director, Agro-chemicals)*

The accounting world is perceived to be changing, not least because the stakes to be won or lost are very large. More managers are judged by results, with a *'P&L responsibility'*, so they take a much closer interest in how their cost centre or divisional results are constructed and how allocated charges can radically alter their perceived performance. But this changing world does not relate just to shifts in professional practice, but also to how the very tools of the accounting trade have undergone massive changes:

> *I look back to costing when I used sheets of analysis paper, a pencil and a rubber. Now it's Lotus or whatever. Twenty years ago I had ten pricing analysts, now I've got two, because their tools are so much slicker they can get data out much faster.*
>
> *(Executive Director, Finance, Motor Manufacturer)*

These brief comments provide a valuable glimpse of the extent to which UK managers perceive management accounting to be changing or that it needs to change. Even though stated in the broadest possible terms they reveal a number of interesting insights, since accounting is clearly perceived to be part of the new wave of management practice. Even when interviewees are not quizzed about it, accounting creeps into their grand new vision of the modern workplace in a most explicit way. Accounting is seen to be intertwined inescapably with the process of organisational change, and we expand this idea through the evidence cited in the remainder of this chapter.

The old ways of accounting and the conventional tools of the craft are no longer perceived to be functional. Seemingly, it is now insufficient simply to suggest modifications at the margin in the ways and tools of accounting. Rather, what is called for now are new ways of accounting and new tools for accountants. As suggested later, UK managers may be too ambitious in their expectations, indeed they may be asking and willing the profession to deliver a number of contradictory demands. But, to their credit, managers appear to be more reflective than the accounting gurus in their appreciation of management accounting's importance in contemporary organisations (Johnson, 1992). We shall return to this theme later, but first we consider the evidence relating to empowerment, accountability, and the accounting function.

7.3 *Empowerment and accountability*

The drive towards greater levels of employee empowerment is seen by UK managers to necessitate increased measures of accountability, and so the two go hand in hand. If lower-level managers are to reap the fruits of self-autonomy and individual initiative, then the scope for opportunism and the possibilities for inefficiency must be checked through increased accountability. Such emphasis on greater accountability seems to be widely spread across our sample and so covers a wide spectrum of industrial classifications. A typical comment is: *'With empowerment comes accountability, so you are accountable for that which you do.' (Operations Manager, Vehicle Assembly)*

Other managers emphasised the emergence of greater accountability in more subtle ways – by, for example, considering the potential problems of autonomy and team working, with the demise of external hierarchical supervision. They conclude that, while *'we can't go round and monitor everything, this is self-monitoring'*, nevertheless such empowerment clearly involves accountability, even if effected through peer pressure.

Whether expressed openly in the most straightforward terms, or dressed up under the guise of self-monitoring and group pressure, interviewees were virtually unanimous in indicating that greater emphasis on accountability has now become commonplace. This is manifested by investment in accounting and management information systems, with the introduction of tighter procedures and demands for more information in greater detail. Such actions are all driven by short-term goals of improving profit by developing quantitative measures of performance – as some managers put it, *'managing by the numbers'*, through an increased use of accounting controls.

In many companies this emphasis on short-termism and bottom-line results was perceived as a manifestation of a deliberate and carefully orchestrated change towards a more calculative style of management. This requires that information now has to be much more accessible and shared at all levels:

> *Policies are more organised and less entrepreneurial. The MD put in a lot of controls inherited from Ford, which we've never seen before. Seat of the pants has changed to a very analytical, carefully controlled management, so we all need information that before was secret to the boss. Now people see the numbers.*
>
> *(Personnel and Commercial Services Director, Motor Dealer)*

With controls and accountability, plus this exposure of lower-level management to information that was previously restricted to the top, comes an increased demand for more detailed, more timely, and more frequent data. Managers reported how teamwork and empowerment meant the shop floor demanded regular monthly profit or performance measures, but in many cases their information systems could not cope and lagged behind.

Some interviewees demonstrated a keen awareness of serious problems that were encountered by their companies as they sought to redesign their accounting systems to facilitate the needs of empowerment and accountability. In some companies there was confusion as to whether the attribution of accountability was meant to be aimed at teams or individuals: *'I think the teams would see accountability as with the team but our mindset still sees it at the individual level.' (Operations Manager, Vehicle Assembly)*

This suggests that, at the operating level, companies have managed to negotiate a shift away from task-centred individualism towards team work. But the structure of decision-making, and with it responsibility, has still remained strongly focused on the individual. In part, this problem appears to be due to a difficulty in partitioning the new organisation into centres of accountability – for example,

> *We try to push accountability out to individuals as it's hard to identify specific asset teams. It's really difficult to know how to carve up the company and look at it from a performance point of view that's actually meaningful and leads to good decision-making. We've struggled with that, it's evolving but we've probably swung a bit too far to the interdependence side, so we're swinging back to a more integrated-type structure.* *(Financial Controller, Oil)*

For this, and other companies, the shift towards team work created new ambiguities relating to identifying what a team is in the first instance. Faced with this uncertainty, some companies seem to find it easier to retain emphasis on individual responsibility. This is, after all, a well-tried and trusted method of accountability in the UK corporate sector.

The recession has emphasised survival and bottom-line results. The resultant tendency to focus on the short term, and possibly compromising longer-term interests, has been noticed by our interviewees. Some were oblique and gentle when expressing their concerns, but others were more explicit:

> *This business and a lot in the UK don't see the writing on the wall because they're too wrapped up in their own market segments and short term results. Management should be looking at least two and three years down the road to identify markets with potential and seeing the writing on the wall well before it hits them.* *(Finance Director, Electronics)*

Hence the tension and potential contradiction between empowerment and accountability, as practised by our interviewees, is manifest in the new wave of management practice. It also translates across to the way in which accounting systems are being redesigned and to the manner of their application. Accounting systems are being called upon to provide more timely, more frequent, and more quantitative information, in order to facilitate the transition towards greater empowerment and accountability. Accounting is also being called upon to partition the new organisation into changed centres of responsibility and calculation, though in attempting to do precisely that, accounting is getting caught up in a new web of challenges:

- How to define new centres of responsibility and accountability that criss-cross different functions.
- How to identify definite boundaries between teams, so that each becomes a clear target for managerial surveillance.
- How to measure the performance of teams, while at the same time promoting an entrepreneurial spirit and motivating the individual members.

Managers are themselves caught in the same contradictions caused by team work practices, while still preoccupied with preserving the culture of individualism. They may therefore be imposing conflicting, or even impossible, burdens on those who are involved in designing and using accounting systems. It may be that the designers can find some scope for evolving a new regime of accountability which can accommodate the new ethos of team work, while yet maintaining the spirit of individualism. Today this is certainly one of the main challenges facing management accountants, both gurus and practitioners.

Yet, irrespective of whether or not this challenge is successfully met, there is another dimension to this argument which may have a most profound implication for management accounting. In an age when empowerment is advocated as the new spirit of the workplace, accounting is seen as the source of the quantitative data used by managers to monitor and discipline employees. Accounting may thus be blamed for providing the opportunity, or even the excuse, for management to abandon the very principles of this involvement and empowerment.

7.4 *Motivation and remuneration*

The role of accounting systems in promoting motivation by linking performance to rewards is well documented, but the focus has tended to be the individual employee. Performance measures were presumed to quantify the achievements of each individual, by comparing actual results against targets to then determine the requisite rewards or sanctions. The new form of organisation poses a new challenge to management accountants. As work is increasingly organised around team work, how can individuals be best motivated to work in the interests of the group?

This question may be seen to represent one of the main aspirations of both accounting system designers and managers. Both are interested in consolidating team spirit, while continuing to reap the benefits of individual entrepreneurship. If such demands are expected to be fulfilled by accounting systems, then many of the premises upon which UK accounting systems are based will have to be fundamentally rethought. Not only this, but it is equally important that managers' attitudes change as regards locating the responsibility and reward.

Our evidence indicates that this challenge is either not recognised or is at best acknowledged, but not addressed. This may be because the motivation and reward issues emerging from the recent changes have not yet become fully clear to practitioners. An alternative and more plausible interpretation would be that practitioners are fully aware of the emerging challenges, but that being inherently difficult to cope with they are deferred, especially if this can be justified by more pressing short-term, day-to-day issues. Either way, the challenges are there and somehow they need to be addressed.

In most researched companies there have been no changes in the reward structure following the emergence of team work: indeed, in many companies it appears that the reward system is not based upon performance. Some companies perceived no need for this during a severe economic recession. There was nevertheless some evidence of variations in reward, which were calculated and managed at the level of the individual: *'Last year we didn't have a general increase; all were individual. A manager will look at relativities and try to ensure it's fair, otherwise employees will become dissatisfied.' (Career Relations and Resourcing Manager, Oil)*

Others appear to avoid the use of performance-related pay, because of their concern over the detrimental effects it can have on the whole company. Some cited problems of needing to be flexible and wanting regularly to revise objectives, but being constrained by a prior linkage of performance-related pay. Selecting particular objectives could also result in an excessive focus on these, to the neglect and detriment of other areas where performance was perfectly acceptable. But even where such reservations were expressed, it seems that performance-related pay is acceptable for senior managers: *'Performance-related pay is a high-level motivator for senior management, so we have recently increased it.' (Managing Director, Agro-chemicals)*

The extent to which performance-related pay is deemed functional varies not only between different companies but, perhaps more interestingly, between different levels within the same company. At one level, most apparently lower-level management, performance-related pay is presumed to be dysfunctional and counter-productive. At top-management level, performance-related pay is perceived as a potent, and an almost inevitable, motivational device.

Various plausible arguments could be made to support this dichotomy, particularly those highlighting the presumed higher levels of skills, crucial centrality to the organisation, and higher mobility of senior managers, as compared with lower levels.

Yet equally plausible counter-arguments can suggest that similar reward schemes should be used at all levels within the same organisation. Our empirical data does not indicate why variations should, or do, exist in rewarding different managerial levels, and this is an important area worthy of more research.

Many of our respondents are so caught up in the web of reward and motivation that they are themselves unclear as to the type of reward scheme used in their company. There is often a confusion between merit, gradings and increments, further compounded when a recession constrains the overall budget and average increases are relatively small. So, perhaps even in those cases where the reward system displays no explicit link to performance, it does tend to mediate pay at the margin. Many companies have been concerned to raise accountability and push it further down the hierarchy, but these two dimensions of accountability and appraisal seem to develop independently of each other: *'Accountability is in place in our operation but what we have not done is to link it to appraisal.' (Customer Services Manager, Financial Services).*

Given that many companies are at a relatively early stage in developing their reward systems, this separation of accountability and reward may be transitory. What is significant from the research, however, is an apparent reluctance to confront the question of team reward. When asked if a team-based reward scheme is on the horizon for her company, the same Customer Services Manager said:

> *No, there's nothing at all on that. But we're the ones making the money or profit and the company had a profit-sharing system. But since overall we're not making a profit as such, obviously we've not got it. Now we've asked at a much higher level for a department reward, and the answer is no.*

Why are companies shying away from confronting the issue of team-based pay? In part, this may be because they are as yet unable to devise a reward system that simultaneously pays the group, while maintaining individual motivation at high levels. For some at least, these two attributes may be inconsistent:

> *We've just put in a person who's responsible for remuneration, it's going to be a big effort next year. But what about functional excellence, for if you really want a remuneration system that says 'I can only succeed if the company succeeds', try going to a salesman and tell him you'll only pay if the company succeeds, not if he gets orders.*
>
> *(Quality and Systems Director, Electronics)*

Functional excellence therefore has a strong pull, being perceived by this manager to run counter to the very essence of group reward. This unmistakable and powerful link with the spirit of individualism, so deeply rooted in our Western culture, was seen in many of the interviews. This electronics company is nevertheless starting to experiment with team-based pay, though on a very small scale. In a pilot experiment they were in the process of introducing what they called self-managed work groups on a functional basis.

Our research thus revealed a number of interesting insights:

- UK managers are aware of the conflict between promoting a team-work culture with the desirability of still being able to pull the motivational levers at the individual level. The problem of 'differentials' does not disappear with the team, especially in a well-established organisation.

- Perhaps because of this culture of individualism, the push towards team-based reward seems to be half-hearted, especially if such pay is seen to be contentious and inconsistent with the espoused ethos of team work and collectivism.
- Presumably for the same reasons, emerging team-based pay systems contradict one of the most fundamental attributes of the new organisation, for they focus on the function, even though the quest for flexibility necessitates moving away from this conventional fixation with specialisms.
- Emerging team-based pay systems also have contradictions when dealing with the remuneration of different levels of management within the same company.
- Recognition that team-based pay may strongly violate the notion of control, on which responsibility accounting is based. How can you fairly reward someone for something they cannot really influence?
- The more fundamental problem of how to measure performance and apply rewards fairly, rather than simply a manager's perception, or the 'blue-eyed boy' syndrome. This is made more difficult when function and line management are separated and tensions created between the gainers and losers.

Some managers claim that they are addressing at least some of these issues by developing new remuneration systems with a different emphasis. One cited *'breadth'*, in the same breath, as *'getting rid of grades altogether'*. But what precisely 'breadth' meant and how it was measured was not made at all clear. Although there is growing recognition by managers that fundamental changes need to be introduced, how to do it is not apparent, only vague suggestions, coupled with self-belief in their ability to confront the problems.

Precisely what kinds of personnel systems and pay schemes would successfully promote team work, and reward such breadth, are yet to be discovered.

An appreciation of the potential problems involved in getting any new scheme to work was apparent, as was a concern that more time might be devoted to devising and managing such schemes than prosecuting the actual business. Some pointed out the problems that car producers had 20 years ago when switching from some sort of piece work to measured day work. There is clearly a risk of espousing the latest fashion, which then gathers its own momentum as if it were an end in itself, divorced from the realities of the workplace, not least the mobility needed to maintain high flexibility. For those with little enthusiasm for group reward there is the discomfort of having seen it all before, and it then being all to no avail.

7.5 *Implications for management accounting*

Many managers see that the management accounting function has been changing in at least two main ways – a significant reduction in accounting personnel and the use of new developments in information technology, which seem to go hand in hand. Even companies that had not heavily focused on computerised information systems were actively exploring the scope for savings, by centralisation and examining documentation. The general drive to reduce costs clearly extended to accounting functions, even before resources were committed to new IT methods.

The evidence also suggests that managers are intent on making radical, rather than incremental, changes in their management information systems (MIS), with the strong conviction that significant advantages will accrue as a result. Others also saw additional advantages of IT at the operational level, through distributed systems, with instant capture and manipulation of performance data. This potentially shifts management accounting from the historical to real time.

For operations management the introduction of new information technology is seen as a major asset that could transform the shop floor. Managers believed it would promote individual initiative; improve planning and expedite production; help to maximise productivity and facilitate both team working and departmental interdependence. Most significantly, it would also potentially increase the scope and scale of management's view into the minute details of the shop floor.

The need for new management information systems is seemingly triggered, not only by the reorganisation of structure, but also by the growth and complexity of activities. Nevertheless, numerous managers, including accountants, see a real scope for making significant reductions in accounting personnel, as for many the world of business is overcrowded by accountants:

The UK is too accounting-oriented compared with Germany or Japan; we're not moving fast enough to reduce it. But I think that causes resentment within the accounting profession, with CIMA and the chartered accountants. Boards are overflowing with accountants, which is a crazy situation, for as an accountant I believe it's one of the reasons why the UK economy is in such a mess [laughter].

(Financial Controller, Agro-chemicals)

As reported in earlier chapters, companies have acted by reducing accounting staff in a dramatic way, linked to innovations in IT. These have, however, tended to be at the clerical end of the operation, perhaps not those in the mind of this Financial Controller. In a number of instances the achievements of Japanese car makers were cited, for example self-billing and automatic payment systems. Yet, despite the apparently impressive actual or potential achievements of IT, many managers expressed reservations, some sharing their bad experiences:

It's been a disaster with breakdowns; our own systems people don't really seem up to it, but we haven't outsourced as yet. I think for security reasons the MD likes it in-house, that's part of the culture.

(Financial Controller, Oil)

So an accounting and technology intervention, when linked to the nature of an organisation's activities or their cultural perception, can make the whole process sensitive to outsiders. The fear is of losing competitive advantage or control, which apparently compels the company to suffer incompetence, as external alternatives are undesirable. Some of the other concerns appeared to be related to age, in that older managers themselves admitted difficulties in adapting to the new world of computerised management accounting systems, or they were unsure about their own and others suitability to be directly involved in operating IT systems:

Older managers, like me, have had more difficulty coming to terms with the computer technology.

(Executive Director, Finance, Motor Manufacturer)

I was always a reluctant IT manager because I never knew much about it and took it over by accident. The main change for me was that I had a hell of a lot more people and they were generally not so bright, so I spent a lot more time managing people.

(Assistant General Manager, Life Customer Services, Financial Services)

This last comment is particularly interesting because it highlights the people aspect, so often overlooked when implementing technicist or system solutions which then fail for the lack of such attention. Well-publicised (even apocryphal) disaster stories raise a concern with managers as to whether the commitment of large resources to IT will actually yield the expected or promised benefits or pay-off.

An emphasis on hardware and the technology of management information systems can undermine rich and complex human relationships by converting them into inadequate yet abstract computer models. Thus the accounting profession has to be aware of such real concerns, as it designs and promotes new systems and practices, if they are heavily reliant upon IT for their implementation.

7.6 Discussion and conclusions

This chapter has indicated some of the implications of changes in management practice for the design and use of accounting systems, but before summarising these it is appropriate to repeat two caveats made in the introduction. Firstly, the research objective was to examine recent changes in management, rather than accounting, practice. Hence the accounting-related evidence upon which we draw is of necessity limited in both scope and depth. Given these unavoidable limitations, the main contribution we hope to make is to raise a number of issues and bring them to the attention of future researchers.

Secondly, our focus is fundamentally different from those previous researchers who have been preoccupied with the technical side of management accounting, and seeking ways of improving the capability of accounting systems to cope with the emerging challenges. In contrast, our focus is upon the embeddedness of accounting in management practices that are changing in response to diverse commercial and (de)regulatory pressures – pressures which are often intensified by these responses. For example, we have sought to shed some light upon how accounting relates to the notions of empowerment and accountability, and how it is caught in the interactions of motivation and remuneration.

Irrespective of their functional specialism, managers acknowledge the central importance of accounting calculations to their everyday activity. Many companies are improving the technical capabilities of their management accounting systems to enhance overall efficiency and effectiveness, especially of costing.

Despite the occasional reference to a need to consider business processes, our sample placed much more emphasis on the monitoring of results. This included putting in standards and controls with auditing to make sure it was happening. This finding, rather than a processual orientation, is apparent in the three themes in the chapter.

Managers extolled the virtues of the employee empowerment programmes their companies had inaugurated, but it has become increasingly obvious that such a process-oriented initiative is on a collision course with the old and trusted model of managing results. Emerging hand in hand with the rhetoric of empowerment is an intensified emphasis on establishing clear lines of command, on evolving modes of accountability with quantitative measures, and on achieving short-term bottom-line results.

Thus management accounting is not being asked to help establish empowerment, either by focusing upon accounting for the processes or by increasing the awareness of interdependence and promoting cross-departmental trust. In fact, we find that the same old (and in a sense precisely opposite) demands of management are still being made – a greater quantification of results, more emphasis on the short term with more frequent and timely information, all for the purposes of monitoring performance.

The link between motivation and remuneration also provides another illustration of an increased emphasis upon managing, and accounting for, results. While the organisation of work has moved inextricably towards building teams and promoting coherent group dynamics, accounting seems to remain hopelessly enmeshed in the old game of seeking to motivate and reward the individual. Hence, in those companies where pay is explicitly related to performance, there is no evidence to suggest that accounting-based remuneration schemes promoting healthy group dynamics are being developed.

Accounting is not simply being passive to the major developments that are shown to be happening in the UK workplace. With some justification, management accounting can stand indicted of inhibiting moves towards the new wave management, because it continues to promote reward schemes that are seen to be in conflict with the aspiration to encourage team work.

The above comments, indicating lack of change in the accounting emphasis, appear to hold, notwithstanding the evidence that the management accounting function has itself recently been undergoing significant changes. These changes seem to be more motivated by the quest for reducing the costs of accounting labour, changes which have been significantly helped by recent developments in information technology. Further, the direct impact that information technology appears to have had on the design of management accounting systems has been restricted to harnessing the new IT to generate yet more quantifiable measures of results and to intensify the monitoring of shop floor by top management.

What is conspicuously absent is evidence to suggest that changes in the management accounting function have been, either wholly or in part, targeted at engineering major changes in the nature of the accounting process itself.

Bibliography

Armstrong, M. (1987), 'Human Resource Management: A Case of the Emperor's New Clothes?', *Personnel Management*, 19, 8.

Armstrong, P. (1989), 'Limits and Possibilities for HRM in an Age of Management Accountancy', in J. Storey (ed.), *New Perspectives on Human Resource Management*, London: Routledge.

Atkinson, P. (1990), *Creating Cultural Change: The Key to Successful Total Quality Management*, Bedford: IFS.

Barney, J.B. (1986), 'Organizational Culture: Can it be a Source of Sustained Advantage?', *Academy of Management Review*, 11, 3.

Beer, M., Spector, B., Lawrence, P.R., Mills, Q.N. and Walton, R.E. (1984), *Managing Human Assets*, New York: Free Press.

Bromwich, M. and Bhimani, A. (1989), *Management Accounting: Evolution Not Revolution*, London: CIMA.

CIMA (1991), *Survey of Management Practices*.

Chandler, A. (1977), *The Visible Hand*, Cambridge, Mass.: Belknap Press.

Clark, J., McLoughlin, I., Rose, H. and King, R. (1988), *The Process of Technological Change*, Cambridge: Cambridge University Press.

Coulson-Thomas, C. and Brown, R. (1989), *The Responsive Organization: People Management, The Challenge of the 1990s*, London: British Institute of Management.

Coulson-Thomas, C. and Brown, R. (1990), *Beyond Quality: Managing the Relationship with the Customer*, London: British Institute of Management.

Coulson-Thomas, C. and Coe, T. (1991), *The Flat Organization*, London: British Institute of Management.

Crosby, P. (1984), *Quality Without Tears: The Art of Hassle-Free Management*, New York: McGraw-Hill.

Cross, M. (1991), 'Monitoring Multiskilling – The Way to Guarantee Long-term Change', *Personnel Management*, 23, 3.

Dahler-Larsen, P. (1991), 'Corporate Culture and Morality: Durkheim-inspired Reflections upon the Limits of Corporate Culture', Working Paper, Department of Economics, University of Odense, Denmark.

Dopson, S., Risk, A. and Stewart, R. (1991), 'The Changing Role of the Middle Manager in the United Kingdom', *International Studies of Management and Organization*, 22, 1.

Dopson, S. and Stewart, R. (1990), 'What is Happening to Middle Management?', *British Journal of Management*, 1.

Drucker, P. (1988), 'The Coming of the New Organization', *Harvard Business Review*, January–February.

Durkheim, E. (1915), *The Elementary Forms of Religious Life: A Study in Religious Sociology*, J.W. Swaim Jr (trans.), London: Allen and Unwin.

Eccleston, B. (1989), *State and Society in Post-war Japan*, Cambridge: Polity.

Edwards, P.K. (1987), *Managing the Factory: A Survey of General Managers*, Oxford: Blackwell.

Ezzamel, M. (1989),'Organisational Change and Behavioural Implications of Change: The Case of Modern Technology', in A. Shahani and R. Stainton (eds), *Tutorial Papers on Operational Research*, Birmingham: Operational Research Society.

Ezzamel, M. (1992), 'Auditor Switches and Auditor Independence', The Maastricht Audit Research Conference, Maastricht, October 1992.

Ezzamel, M. and Hart, H. (1987), *Advanced Management Accounting*, London: Cassell.

Ezzamel, M., Hoskin, K. and Macve, R. (1990), 'Managing It All By Numbers: A Review of Johnson and Kaplan's "Relevance Lost"', *Accounting and Business Research*, 78, Spring.

Fitzgerald, T.H. (1988), 'Can Change in Organizational Culture Really Be Managed?', *Organizational Dynamics*, Autumn.

Foucault, M. (1978), *The History of Sexuality, Vol. 1: An Introduction*, London: Allen Lane.

Foucault, M. (1980), *Power/Knowledge*, C. Gordon (ed), Brighton: Harvester.

Friedman, A.L. (1977), *Industry and Labour*, London: Macmillan.

Gilbert, N. and Burrows, R. (1992), *Fordism and Flexibility*, London: Macmillan.

Goffee, R. and Scase, R. (1986), 'Are the Rewards Worth the Effort? Changing Managerial Values in the 1980s', *Personnel Review*, 15.

Goldsmith, W. and Clutterbuck, D. (1984), *The Winning Streak*, London: Weidenfeld and Nicholson.

Guest, D.E. (1987), 'Human Resource Management and Industrial Relations', *Journal of Management Studies*, 24, 5.

Guest, D.E. (1990), 'Human Resource Management and the American Dream', *Journal of Management Studies*, 27, 4

Guest, D.E. (1991), 'Personnel Management: The End of Orthodoxy?', *British Journal of Industrial Relations*, 29, 2.

Gunz, H. and Whitley, R. (1985), 'Managerial Cultures and Industrial Strategies in British Firms', *Organization Studies*, 6, 3.

Handy, C. (1989), *The Age of Unreason*, London: Business Books.

Harvey, D. (1989), *The Condition of Post-Modernity*, Oxford: Blackwell.

Hendry, C. and Pettigrew, A. (1990), 'Human Resource Management: An Agenda for the Nineties', *International Journal of Human Resource Management*, 1, 1.

Hendry, C., Pettigrew, A. and Sparrow, P. (1988), 'Changing Patterns of Human Resource Management', *Personnel Management*, 20, 11.

Hill, S. (1990), 'How Do You Manage a Flexible Firm? The Total Quality Model', *Work, Employment and Society*, 5, 3.

Hill, S. (1991), 'Why Quality Circles Failed but Total Quality Might Succeed', *British Journal of Industrial Relations*, December.

Johnson, H.T. (1992), 'Relevance Revisited: Total Quality Management and the Role of Management Accounting', *Critical Perspectives on Accounting*, in press.

Johnson, H.T. and Kaplan, R.S. (1987), *Relevance Lost*, Boston: Harvard University Press.

Kanter, R.M. (1984), *The Change Masters*, London: Allen and Unwin.

Kanter, R.M. (1989), 'The New Managerial Work', *Harvard Business Review*, November–December.

Kanter, R.M. (1990), *When Giants Learn to Dance*, London: Unwin Hyman.

Kaplan, R.S. (1983), 'Measuring Manufacturing Performance: A New Challenge for Managerial Accounting Research', *The Accounting Review*, October.

Kaplan, R.S. (1984) 'The Evolution of Management Accounting', *The Accounting Review*, July.

Keenoy, T. (1990a), 'HRM: A Case of the Wolf in Sheep's Clothing?', *Personnel Review*, 19, 2.

Keenoy, T. (1990b), 'Review Article: Human Resource Management – Rhetoric, Reality and Contradiction', *International Journal of Human Resource Management*, 1, 3.

Keenoy, T. and Anthony, P. (1992), 'HRM: Metaphor, Meaning and Morality' in P. Blyton and P. Turnbull (eds), *Reassessing Human Resource Management*, London: Sage.

Kerfoot, D. and Knights, D. (1992), 'Managerial Evangelism: Planning for Quality in Financial Services', Working Paper, Manchester School of Management.

Kerfoot, D. and Knights, D. (in press), 'Planning for Personnel? Human Resource Management Reconsidered', *Journal of Management Studies.*

Killman, R.H., Saxton, M.J., Serpa, R. (eds) (1985), *Gaining Control of the Corporate Culture*, San Francisco: Jossey-Bass.

Knights, D. and Willmott H.C. (1987), 'Organizational Culture as Management Strategy', *International Studies of Management and Organization*, XVII, 3.

Knights, D. and Willmott, H.C. (1988), 'The Executive Fix: Strategic Decision Making in the Financial Services Industry' in J. McGoldrick (ed.), *Business Case File on Behavioural Science Students*, Wokingham: Van Nostrand Reinhold.

Knights, D. and Willmott, H.C. (1992), 'Conceptualising Leadership Processes: A Study of Senior Managers in a Financial Services Company', *Journal of Management Studies.*

Knights, D. and Willmott, H.C. (1993), '"It's a Very Foreign Discipline": The Genesis of Expenses Control in a Mutual Life Company', *British Journal of Management.*

Kunda, G. (1992), *Engineering Culture: Control and Commitment in a High-Tech Corporation*, Philadelphia: Temple University Press.

Lash, S. and Urry, J. (1987), *The End of Organizational Capitalism*, Cambridge: Polity Press.

Legge, K. (1989), 'Human Resource Management: A Critical Analysis', in J. Storey (ed), *New Perspectives on Human Resource Management*, London: Routledge.

Lester, T. (1992), 'Metamorphosis of the Manager', *Management Today*, August.

Locke, C. (1989), *Higher Education since 1940*, Cambridge: Cambridge University Press.

Merchant, K.A. (1987), *Rewarding Results*, Boston, Mass: Harvard Business School Press.

Miles, R.E. and Snow, C.C. (1978), *Organizational Strategy*, Structure and Process, London: McGraw-Hill.

Morgan, G. (1988), *Riding the Waves of Change: Developing Managerial Competencies for a Turbulent World*, London: Sage.

Morishima, M. (1984), *Why Has Japan Succeeded?*, Cambridge: Cambridge University Press.

Oakland, J. (1989), *Total Quality Management*, London: Heinemann.

Ouchi, W.G. (1981), *Theory Z: How American Business Can Meet the Japanese Challenge*, New York: Addison-Wesley.

Pascale, R.T. (1991), *Managing on the Edge: How Successful Companies Use Conflict to Stay Ahead*, Harmondsworth: Penguin.

Peppercorn, G. and Skoulding, G. (1987), *Profile of British Industry: The Manager's View*, London: British Institute of Management.

Peters, T.J. (1988), *Thriving On Chaos; Handbook for a Management Revolution*, London: Macmillan.

Peters, T.J. (1989), *Thriving on Chaos*, London: Pan.

Peters, T.J. (1992), 'Managing Change: An Oxymoron?', Paper presented at a business conference on 'The Management of Change', London.

Peters, T. and Austin, N. (1986), *A Passion for Excellence*, London: Fontana.

Peters, T.J. and Waterman, R.H. (1982), *In Search of Excellence: Lessons from America's Best-run Companies*, New York: Harper and Row.

Pettigrew, A.M. (1985), *The Awakening Giant: Continuity and Change at ICI*, Oxford: Basil Blackwell.

Pettigrew, A. and Whipp, R. (1991), *Managing Change for Competitive Success*, Oxford: Basil Blackwell/ESRC.

Piore, M. and Sabel, C. (1984), *The Second Industrial Divide: Possibilities for Prosperity*, New York: Basic Books.

Pollert, A. (1987), 'The "Flexible Firm": A Model in Search of Reality (or a Policy in Search of a Practice)?', *Warwick Papers in Industrial Relations*, 19.

Pollert, A. (ed) (1991), 'Farewell to Flexibility?', *Warwick Studies in Industrial Relations*, Oxford: Blackwell.

Ray, C.A. (1984), 'Corporate Culture: The Last Frontier of Control', *Journal of Management Studies*, 23, 3.

Robbins, S.P. (1983), 'The Theory Z Organization from a Power-Control Perspective', *Californian Management Review*, XXV, 25.

Sewell, G. and Wilkinson, B. (1992), 'Empowerment Or Emasculation? A Tale of Workplace Surveillance in the Total Quality Organization', in P. Blyton and P. Turnbull (eds), *Human Resource Management: Conflicts and Contradictions*, London: Sage.

Sisson, K. (1990), 'Introducing the Human Resource Management Journal', *Human Resource Management Journal*, 1, 1.

Smith, C., Child, J. and Rowlinson, M. (1991), *Reshaping Work: Cadbury Experience*, Cambridge: Cambridge University Press.

Smith, V. (1990), *Managing in the Corporate Interest: Control and Resistance in an American Bank*, Berkeley: University of California Press.

Smith, D., and Harbisher, A (1989), 'Building Societies as Retail Banks: The Importance of Customer Service and Corporate Image', *International Journal of Bank Marketing*, 7, 1

Soeters, J.L. (1986), 'Excellent Companies as Social Movements', *Journal of Management Studies*, 23, 3.

Starkey, K. and McKinlay, A. (1988), *Organizational Innovation: Competitive Strategy and the Management of Change in Four Major Companies*, Aldershot: Avebury.

Torrington, D. (1989), 'Human Resource Management and the Personnel Function' in J. Storey (ed.), *New Perspectives on Human Resource Management*, London: Routledge.

Torrington, D. and Hall, L. (1987), *Personnel Management: A New Approach*, London: Prentice Hall International.

Townley, B. (forthcoming), 'Foucault, "Power-Knowledge" and its Relevance for HRM', *Academy of Management Review*.

Van Maanen, J. (1992), 'The Smile Factory: Work at Disneyland' in Frost, P.J. Moore, L.F., Louis, M.L., Lundberg, C.C. and Martin, J., *Reframing Organizational Culture*, London: Sage.

Waterman, R.H. (1988), *The Renewal Factor*, New York: Bantam.

Watson, T. (1977), *The Personnel Managers*, London: Routledge.

Wheatley, M. (1992), *The Future of Middle Management*, London: British Institute of Management.

Whipp, R. and Clark, P. (1986), *Innovation and the Auto Industry: Product, Process and Work Organization*, London: Pinter.

Whittaker, A. (1992), 'The Transformation in Work: Post-Fordism Revisited' in Reed, M. and Hughes, M. (eds), *Rethinking Organisation: New Directions in Organizational Theory and Analysis*, London: Sage.

Whittington, R. (1989), *Corporate Strategies in Recession and Recovery: Social Structure and Strategic Choice*, London: Unwin Hyman.

Wilkinson, A. (1992), 'The Other Side of Quality: "Soft" Issues and the Human Resource Dimension', *Total Quality Management*, 3, 3.

Wilkinson, A., Allen, P. and Snape, A. (1991), 'TQM and the Management of Labour', *Employee Relations*, 13, 1.

Wilkinson, A., Marchington, M. and Goodman, J. (1992), 'Total Quality Management and Employee Involvement', *Human Resource Management Journal*, 2, 4.

Willmott, H.C. (1992), 'Post-Modernism and Excellence: The De-differentiation of Economy and Culture', *Journal of Organisational Change Management*, 5, 1.

Willmott, H.C. (forthcoming), 'Strength Is Ignorance, Slavery is Freedom: Managing Culture in Modern Organizations', *Journal of Management Studies*.

Wood, S. (1989), 'New Wave Management?', *Work, Employment and Society*, 3, 3.